The Art of the
INSURANCE
DEAL

The Art of the Insurance Deal
Copyright © 2018 Jeff Arnold

RIGHTSURE PUBLISHING

Book design by:
Arbor Services, Inc.
www.arborservices.co/

Printed in the United States of America

The Art of the Insurance Deal
Jeff Arnold

1. Title 2. Author 3. Business

Library of Congress Control Number: 2017917508
ISBN 13: 978-0-692-98206-8

The Art of the
INSURANCE
DEAL

JEFF ARNOLD

RIGHTSURE PUBLISHING

If our paths have crossed, you have taught me something and I am grateful

This book is dedicated to
Laura Lee, Jafe, Brock, Braeden and Callie Anne

Contents

Introduction

Down at the Del

"There are no ordinary moments."
Socrates

My in-laws, my kids, and my wife were all there to celebrate Christmas into New Year's 2000 at San Diego's luscious Hotel Del Coronado, but I couldn't get out of bed. No, I didn't have the flu. I was healthy, wise, and even a bit wealthier than usual. But I skipped most of the meals and all the events that week, even though my wife's family had come in from Florida, Arizona, Mexico, and Colorado; I'd prove to be antisocial with a capital A, although I didn't want to be.

I kept the curtains pulled tight in the room, lights off. I loved these people. I had been looking forward to this time away, the Del Coronado is spectacular (it is the hotel that *Some Like It Hot* was filmed at), and as I say, financially things were pretty good in our lives currently because of a deal I had just managed. I should have been celebrating. I should have been on top of the world. I should have, at the very least, gotten up for dinner once or twice.

But I was down for the count.

It wasn't postpartum depression, but man it felt like it! A complete and utter body-numbing malaise had come up to grab me that week after selling my insurance business. Having run my agency for eight

1

years, I never realized—until I sold it—how much my identity was wrapped up in what I did every day, and if the way I was feeling that New Year's week was any indication, it seemed I still needed to be at my agency's helm to feel alive. Yes, I came through the front door and I was husband and father, I was a brother to my siblings and son to my folks, but so much of my life, I was coming to realize with this body-aching numbness, was about running my business that I so loved.

And now, I didn't have it anymore.

I sold my insurance agency in late 1999 to a mortgage bank. Part of my deal in selling was that not only would I receive a cash settlement (a nice chunk of change back then, but not enough to set my family and me up for life), I'd also be kept on for five years as a highly paid executive. But I guess seeing as I was full fetal during that holiday break, I was having a hard time reconciling the me right then with the me I would become.

Not that I could have articulated what was swirling 'round the old dull organ that was my brain right then. All these deeply seated concerns and questions of my identity were beyond my conscious reach at the time. I just knew I was having a hard time dealing with it all, and my kids were pretty much at their wit's end, constantly at my wife with, "Um, so what's wrong with Dad?"

Things would work out fine, in time. I would go on to work hard and reap the reward of doing so for that same bank who bought my agency. I'd quickly become a highly paid executive in the company, jetting here and there, the recipient of a healthy expense account, getting more than slightly carried away with myself, if truth be told.

I'd come to work hand in hand with the CEO and CFO of the bank acquiring other insurance agencies—my initial idea—growing a skill that would truly prove valuable to me in my future. I'd even come to run a division overseeing two hundred employees. With the money I received from the sale of my agency I even started my sons (I had two at the time) on their way to learning and investing in stocks. I'd come to teach them an important lesson, that one should invest in businesses one has an interest in, that one likes. (My one son loved Apple products at the time, so he ended up doing quite well. My other son chose Sony and, though the stock didn't fare as well, he too learned the basics of investing at a young age.)

As you may remember, the bottom fell out of the banking business in 2008, and even though by that time I was living the aforementioned corporate dream, I found myself suddenly out of a job. Buying back my agency from the bank (for double the price that I had sold it), I got back into the insurance business, not without a small bit of wrangling, which I will tell you about later. And the comeback has been a blessing every single day since.

So from curled up in bed at the Del to once again master of my destiny, I came to see the many weird and wonderful twists the roads of life can take us.

"Giver of life, dream fulfiller, an industry of all things sexy, exciting and just plain awesome," this is part of the quote we have scrolling across my personal website and what I truly believe about the insurance business. As you will come to see, I have a strong spiritual background. My core belief informs my view that what we do in the insurance business is important to sustaining the substance of who we are—for what people need in their lives, how we protect our families, and all the positive changes we can manage in our futures. The success I have enjoyed in the insurance business has gone beyond my wildest dreams, and how I have come to affect people's lives for the better brings me joy every day.

For the past years of heading the RIGHTSURE Insurance Group, I have been as much interested in selling insurance as I have been in acquiring other agencies, and those acquisitions have steered RIGHTSURE into a future I've envisioned for the company. After selling the agency I owned, then buying it back years later; having worked hard from the ground up in an industry I never knew about until I started in it and having made quite a success in it; having come to see so many different types of brokerages and insurance companies and how they interact, for good or for bad, I feel I am in a unique position to be sympathetic as a broker buyer.

I also know the ins and outs of selling. What the seller needs to consider even before he or she puts feelers out to a company like mine is certainly what to do to make your agency as lucrative an acquisition as it can be.

But I'm not writing this book just to hear myself talk. Yes, I'm a salesman by nature; I can talk a blue streak with the best of them. But the reason I wrote this book you are holding in your hands is that in the past five years I have seen an exodus tsunami of insurance agency owners. In their early sixties or slightly older, so many of the men and women who have worked and built the American insurance business through the past four decades have come to the end of their tethers. They are looking to finally fully enjoy that villa on the beach they bought that they only got to take their spouse to a couple of times a year. They are hoping now to get much more time with the grandkids. They want to realize their dream of renting an RV and finally getting to those spots across the country they never had time to get to, or better yet, buying a couple of Harleys and suiting up with the Mr. or the Mrs. and taking to the open road . . . Heck, I'm right here ready to insure those rides!

As we are all well aware, no matter how much money you made, how many toys you may have been able to buy your family, how comfortable your life became from running your business—no matter what kind of a business you were in—you had to have spent an enormous amount of time and effort to grow your little piece of the pie. And I know, especially, working this "industry of all things sexy, exciting, and just plain awesome," you needed to give your shop your constant attention. You might have a staff of two or fifty, everybody in place doing one particular job and doing it well, but at the end of the day, all responsibility falls on your shoulders. You had to have been ever aware of the changes slicing through the market at any given time, in how people lived their lives, how the competition was acting. After awhile, certainly in your sixth decade, you could come to tire of even the greatest job of all time.

You might also be one of those folks I see who simply wants to get out of the business end of things but wants to keep selling insurance. You're not exactly tired of the work. In fact, you like it, but man you are tired of worrying about the business. You're seeking a buyer who will buy you out over a period but who will let you keep selling insurance and making deals.

If you have an inkling that you are coming to the end, in whatever way you want to come to it, are putting the pieces in place to sell, or are simply looking for some pointers in how to consider your agency anew . . . read on. If you simply like reading about others like you, in the same field, who approach what we do with a no-nonsense approach . . . read on. If you might well connect with someone from humble beginnings who has made a grand success in insurance . . . read on. Or if you are looking for a buyer right now . . . read on.

Chapter 1

Bio: The Kentucky Kid

"Light yourself on fire with passion and people will come from miles to watch you burn."
John Wesley (1703–1791)

A Norman Rockwell painting come to life was my life growing up in the early seventies in Cadiz, Kentucky. In this small suburb of Hopkinsville, I grew up a skinny kid with a shock of red hair who played outside until dinnertime, left doors unlocked, and was surrounded by my loving family. I was the middle child, and like most middle children, I was always second to the superior skills and athleticism of my older brother Michael Shane. My younger sister, Glynanna Michelle, is as pretty as her name. My brother and sister were my best friends growing up. I come from a background of Baptist ministers—my grandfather and his father before him were ordained, and if my dad hadn't liked cars so much, he would have been a minister as well. As it was, my father was deeply involved in the church on many levels, and we were regular church-goers to be sure.

Faith loomed large in my life, as it still does, but forget some of the modern- day prejudices born from hearing about people using Baptist beliefs for hate-filled aims. Any solid, life-affirming ethos, empowering philosophy, and worldview can be too easily perverted by folks with evil hearts. What I learned from my faith and took to heart on a regular basis were the simple concepts of being humble and approaching life with love for my fellow man, no matter who he (or she) happens to be and what they believe (or don't) believe. Yes, as Baptists we are called to testify, and certainly, coming from the background I did, I witnessed many fire-and-brimstone sermons growing up.

But even though I consider my faith the most important anchor in my life, a living, breathing light in my soul, heart, and mind, I have never been one of those people who felt that anybody else need believe what I do. I even told each of my kids as they entered their teens that they would need to come to their own conclusions over the specific challenges they would face in life. How they felt about alcohol (and other like substances), how they felt about money and how they would come to deal with it, and even how they built a relationship with God, if at all, had to be on them. I think I learned this somewhere back in my growing up from my grandfather, a Baptist preacher to be sure, but a man who understood that every person is on a journey and must experience things in their life in their way and in their own time.

I maintain this hands-off attitude with my employees, often to the frustration of my managers. When the leadership of RIGHTSURE is pushing for change or for our agents to do things a certain way (ever notice how a manager never sees those things that might need changing in his or her self?), there is bound to come some friction. I don't want confrontation, though I don't fear it, but I will make my feelings known (this is my company, after all) that I will continue to display and act from a platform of infinite patience with how my employees grow and come to their own conclusions. Jamming your worldview down someone's throat usually ends up causing gagging (friction); I am a more a forest-for-the-trees kind of a leader. When it comes to what I believe, in the office as much as in my faith, I go my way without agenda, try to give good counsel when asked for it (and only when asked), and try to accept people for who they are.

Besides, you hire people for what you see in them, for their abilities, potential, what they bring to your office or store. Why sit on them and micromanage their approach? I can learn as much as teach, can't I?

Now, as much as Dad loved our faith, as I said, he also had a deep passion for cars. This led him to work for my mom's dad in his garage after a chance meeting at, where else?—CHURCH—fated him coming in contact with my mom.

My mother's family was entrepreneurs before that word was invented. Her father owned a combination auto garage/gas station/saw mill; he was the town's "Mr. Fix-It," and rumor had it that her family were superb moonshiners. All I knew was that they were wonderful people with rich traditions and incredible stories to tell. The connection between the good ole boys running illegal alcohol—alcohol that could as much fuel their souped-up cars as a good blind drunk—and racing fast cars is the stuff of true American legend. As they were always trying to outdrive the law in ever-faster cars, the moonshiners took to racing one other after a time, just men growing bored and itching to show off, I guess. After even more time somebody came to cut a crude track through a cow pasture.

The rest is NASCAR history.

Was it any wonder my father, with his love of cars, would take to a girl who came from such a rich tradition?

We were lower middle class, but I don't recall ever considering this distinction or wanting for anything. I worked as soon as I was able—at fourteen bailing hay on Mr. Newton's farm Saturdays for $10 a day—a work ethic instilled in me early on that if I wanted something I'd have to work for it. In fact, it was during one of those brutally hot afternoons as I came to be standing in the dusty barn on a hay bale that I was first introduced to the insurance business.

A man drove up in a four-door Buick . . . with the windows up, meaning he had air conditioning! When he got out, all crisp and clean—not sweating a drip—in his starched white shirt, this seemingly expensively appointed guy made such an impression on me, I remember asking the worker next to me: "What's that guy do?" to which I was told: "Insurance."

I am sure this left a lasting impression on me of the possible riches to be had in a profession that I hadn't, up until then, even knew existed.

When I was four, my mom and dad divorced. I vividly remember crying on the front stoop as my father gathered his things and left the house for good. In the early 70s this was a big deal, and for a family with such a deep connection to God, my parents' divorcing was something that instantly stigmatized my family. And that kind of news spread fast in the small town we lived in, believe me! But my mother, brother, and sister, who was only one at the time, soldiered on.

How my mom raised three kids, kept a roof over our head, fed, and clothed us, I'll never know. I look at my life now, my wife and four kids and all that we have, how well we live from the good fortunes we've had, and I can't conceive of how we survived way back when without my father and from what little my mother brought in from her work. Still, we had Atari and our "pong" game. We had bicycles, clean clothes, food, and though we didn't see Dad all that much, didn't attend his church so much after the divorce, he still came by, and my brother, sister, and I maintained a good relationship with him. We'd drive an hour once a week and visit my mom's family in the deep country, stay the weekend sometimes, and life went on. Only later, as I will relate in a bit, did I come to realize that we were living a lower-middle-class existence in Kentucky and that, indeed, we were a minority in a quickly desegregating area of town.

Tulsa

About four years after her divorce, my mom remarried. My stepdad was a career military man, and he soon moved my mom and my siblings and me to Tulsa, OK. Wow, talk about an eye-opener! Here is where I first realized that there were classes in the U.S . . . and not only classes in school. In Tulsa I saw lots of kids who had moms who stayed home, didn't work at all, made nice lunches for their children, and had nobody in the family on a school meal plan. In my new surroundings, where white people were the majority, I came to learn what opulence meant. My brother, sister, and I each had our own rooms. How cool was that?

I had never been a great student. From grammar school on up, the best you could say about my scholastic achievements was that they were consistently mediocre. I played percussion in the school band, and I took to drama and anything of a more creative bent, but academics would never be my strong suit. I was a bright kid, well-liked, sociable enough, but studying wasn't ever going to be my thing. School in Tulsa was certainly harder than it had been in Kentucky, and I barely broke a C average after our move. I was more interested in sweeping up the local pizza parlor (I'd come to work all throughout high school, my work ethic always going strong), making some money, rather than hitting the books.

Even before graduation, I had enlisted in the army, as much probably from my stepdad's influence as the fact that I had no place else to go after graduation. My mom and stepdad didn't have the means to send my siblings and me on for further education, so college wasn't a topic and had never even been discussed around our dinner table. Even now I don't particularly feel deprived that I wasn't able to further my education; I wasn't the best student at that point anyway. Besides, as you will see, the army opened me up to learning in a way I couldn't have ever dreamed.

The Army and Coming into My Own

I took basic training at Fort Leonard Wood in Missouri, and from the get-go I excelled. I matured in the army; that's really the only word for it. Maybe it was the regimentation. Maybe it was living on my own for the first time in my life. Maybe I simply took to the specific things they were teaching me. All I know is that I came into my own those first few months in the service.

After basic training, I was stationed at Fort Gordon in Georgia, and with my regular assignment set, I thrived even more. I began to learn about 35K Aviation Electronics, working on navigation, night vision goggles, and electronic equipment in specially designed helicopters for a new Special Ops unit of the United States Army and a single National Guard unit in Oklahoma. This new technology would become crucial to the U.S. military.

When I think back over what we were doing with that burgeoning technology, I am reminded of the Billy Joel song "Goodnight Saigon." The lyrics sum up the military's reaction post-Vietnam, where the U.S. military felt defenseless against the North Vietnamese at night. The powers that be in the military decided that U.S. troops would never again come up short because they couldn't navigate at night. "We will own the night," became a mantra I heard often, and regardless of the budget, the military began developing night-vision goggles and technology—stuff you can go out and buy today at any sporting goods store. We were just coming off the rescue attempt of Operation Desert One, where U.S. helicopters crashed in the night and all but got lost in Iran. "Death comes at night" if you weren't ready for it. The army was strictly set on getting the best they could out of us technicians working on the most sophisticated instruments available for a sure goal.

I was being taught how to care for and repair all the latest in night vision goggles, being schooled on all this top-secret stuff. I loved it.

I had a feeling of being set on an important purpose, and this sense of working hard on this task of the highest priority, being part of the team in this way, and being a master of myself and my time, all worked wonders on my self-confidence and psyche. Suddenly, I began doing something I could never have dreamed of doing before . . . spending my nights and weekends, basically all my time off, in the post library.

It had been a chore for me to crack open a textbook back in high school. I could probably count on one hand how many times I had walked into a library while growing up. My reading comprehension was fine, but I certainly hadn't used it all that much, beyond maybe reading a magazine or a newspaper; books were not exactly kryptonite to me, but they had never been close companions. But there I was spending all my free time in the library, around all those books, and loving it. I devoured everything I read, and I read everything, flittering from one subject to another, not able to satiate my curiosity. I had never had, nor had I ever cultivated a thirst for knowledge in this way, but spending all that time in the library I could feel my mind expanding, and I loved it.

I guess you could say I grew up through the responsibilities given me, the challenges I faced with such important work and the more I opened myself up to a better education—self-teaching myself as I was. Thus I began to take more responsibility in what I did with my life. And educating myself was something I realized was of the utmost importance.

I was in for three and half years, and although I was learning a lot, I was ready to move on at the end of my time. I don't exactly know when the realization hit me, but suddenly I knew I had to get out, regardless of how much I liked where I was, how important my work was, how much I was learning, and how I had the run of the place and had my life ordered just the way I liked it. I applied for the early leave the army was offering at the time and left the service to get on with a new chapter of my life.

Tucson

I moved to Tucson, AZ, where my mom and stepfather now lived. Regrouping in their house as much as decompressing from army life, I figured out my next move.

While in the army I had taken and done well on a skills test. From those results, I was told that I could have a pick of what I wanted to do, that I could excel at pretty much anything. But I had no idea exactly what that was. But the G.I. bill was there to pay for my college books, and with my new thirst for learning, I enrolled in the junior college near our house, taking acting and drama classes and fitting back into civilian life. I also acted in a few in-class productions and even began getting up for some open mike stand-up at local comedy clubs. If you want to face real fear and conversely grow your confidence, get up and do stand-up for a while; that was more hair-raising than anything I ever faced in army training! But even coaxing the smallest laugh from a barely attentive audience will feed an addiction for the stage you can't ignore.

After two years in Tucson, I moved to California with two of my buddies to a place my uncle let us have for free. I was going to try and work my way into the professional world of stand-up, above and beyond what I had tried in Tucson. Make no mistake about it; the early 90s was a wild time to be in Hollyweird. I could write another book on the stuff I saw during that time. It was pretty much a nonstop party (none of which I really took to), with lots of rich kids spending money like crazy, and guys like me writing jokes during the day, trying to get on a stage at night, any stage, to do five minutes and catch some club owner's attention to maybe land an opening set. Guys and girls got chewed up and spit out, and some actually made it, at least what we considered making it back then. My life was a whirlwind. I did OK, got some gigs, made some contacts, but after ten months of taking my shot, I knew I wasn't going to go anywhere with that particular dream.

And I needed money, quick.

My First Agency

Boomeranging back to Tucson to stay with my mom and stepdad again, I looked for a job. I came to answer an ad to work at a local insurance agency though I had no aspirations for that business, no thoughts about it at all really . . . except maybe that memory from way back when, seeing that insurance man in his crisp shirt stepping out of that fancy car when I was bailing hay. But I went down to the office and got the job. Later on, I would come to learn from the ladies who worked at that office, many of whom I would come to hire for my agency, that they went to the boss and told him to "hire that guy" after I left. I guess the confidence I had built from all that stand-up, my quick wit, the fact that I knew enough to look people in the eye when engaging in a conversation with them, my gregariousness, and the fact that I truly like people made me somebody the boss felt worth hiring.

The agency was a high-risk vehicle insurer, and I jumped in with both feet. Of course, I had no idea what high-risk vehicle insurance meant. But I quickly learned all about writing policies for people who had lost their license at one time or maybe accrued other violations so firms like State Farm or Farmers would not want to insure them. God knows, lots of folks of all ages, ethnicities, and genders are "risky" to insure for a whole host of reasons, and you come in contact with a lot of these folks when insuring cars and motorcycles.

I took to that job. I loved it, actually. I was then, and probably will always be, a quintessential "people person," and selling insurance, especially niche insurance, you come into contact with people all the time. Pretty quickly, though, I began to think, *Heck, Jeff, you could do this for yourself. You could be selling insurance through your own agency.* There is a fine line between confidence and foolishness, I know, but I kept the idea that I might indeed strike out on my own simmering on the back burner of those slow-turning windmills of my mind those first few months, working and learning as much as I could.

As luck would have it, during my first few weeks at the agency, a salesman, John Adams, came into our office trying to get us to carry Colonial Insurance Of California. As you may not be aware, smaller carriers—and Colonial was smaller; they didn't have any brand name recognition at the time—literally come knocking on an agency's doors all the time. I get them coming to RIGHTSURE constantly. Sure, I have been on the other end of that equation as a smaller broker just starting out; I was the one "come a-courtin'" the bigger carriers on a regular basis.

A funny story is how it took me four years to convince Safeco to let me sell them, and this was years later when my agency was established. I had to solicit them for three years before they even would welcome a proposal from me. I printed and bound in leather a fifty-page business plan for them, back in the day when you did such things, and still it took me five months for them to send somebody down to see me and another year before they agreed to let me represent them. All that work paid off in the end, as Safeco is always a top three carrier in our firm. I'd come to know how tough this grind is, cold selling with a product that isn't yet proven.

Back to John, who was deep in that grind. He was a nice silver-haired gentleman wearing crisp short sleeves, at least ten years older than most other salesman in the game. Suffice it to say, nobody in my agency would meet with the guy. The climate in my office was that of a Wall Street shop filled with young, high-energy agents looking to make their next big score. Men and women alike who thought they were too cool for school, who couldn't be taught a thing certainly didn't have time for John. This image didn't fit me. I was too green to have ever considered myself that hip and cool, even if I had wanted to; I was out of place with all those hotshot hip insurance agents, and glad to be so. John was out of place too, as much because of his age as with his old-school pocket-protector-in-his-pocket style.

Of course I sat down with the man.

As you've read, I am a social guy. I like to learn someone's story if I have the time, even these days when my time is taken up by so much daily business. Besides, as I've found time and again, sharing a moment or a coffee with somebody I often learn so much. John and I got along like a house on fire covered with good insurance. He had lots to teach me about the business, and like a sponge, I soaked up his wisdom as he gave me his pitch. And although I told him I did not make decisions at the office, couldn't even put in a good word for Colonial (not that anybody would have listened to me, being as new as I was), we got along famously, and at the end of the meeting he gave me his card.

When I came to leave the agency and step out on my own, who do you think I called to be my first—and for a long time only—carrier?

The happenstance of meeting John that day speaks to a couple of big lessons I have come to learn and have seen played out time and again: 1) Never burn a bridge, and 2) It pays to be nice to people and give them, at the very least, the time of day.

Jeff Arnold Insurance was born when I left the agency two months later. I bought two metal file cabinets, stretched a wooden plank door across them to make a desk, and installed a phone line in the office of my mother's house, which was pretty much an unused closet space. White Pages in hand, I began cold calling, selling policies for Colonial Insurance Of California, my flagship brand. I calculated that I could just cover my expenses and reach the modest salary I wanted by making two hundred calls a day and writing nineteen policies a month, which I would do in time, but it took me three and half months to make those projected nineteen deals. Remember, this was well before the days of online tutorials. There wasn't any place to go to get training other than working for an agency, which I had just come from. I couldn't scour the Internet at night for insurance news groups, there was no HowToBuildAndRunYourNewInsuranceAgencyJeff.com. I had to motivate myself and get on with the getting on of the work. This was pure telecommuting—picking up the phone, a landline can you believe it?—before that term was born.

As you can suspect, I still remember my first sale. I was calling all over Tucson, not paying attention to zip codes, when I happened to get lucky and connect to a woman who had just bought a motorcycle for her son. She was looking almost exactly at that second I called for someone to insure the bike. She told me I'd need to come to her to seal the deal, so I did, driving to the bank she worked in, located clear across the city from my "office." All told, when you subtract how much it cost me in gas to drive back and forth and sign her to that motorcycle policy, I probably made a commission of eleven dollars on that first signing, netting essentially no money.

But I was on my way.

I was still in high-risk insuring. Colonial was a vehicle insurer, selling all kinds of policies for all kinds of vehicles. This is where the "sexiness" of insurance came for me—learning the nuances of writing policies to cover cars and boats and motorcycles was interesting and, at times, creative work. And if it was cool when I was working for the agency, it was super James Bond slick when working for myself—massaging deals and making plays on my own dime. Each person you come to insure, especially with high-risk policies, has a unique story, a specific set of circumstances that got them to where they need the specific policy they do. You have to finagle, work numbers, figure details—get creative—to try and get your potential insured the best policies you can so they will sign with you. And let's face it, a boat is not a car is not a motorcycle is not a spaceship. I would have loved to try and figure out a policy for a spaceship!

I hit the ground running every day, not knowing what was going to be thrown my way and wanting to experience it all.

I worked hard, and my business grew. After three months I finally managed enough clients that I could move to an actual office. I rented space in a professional building and hired my sister, who was taking time off between graduating from high school and starting college, as my first employee. She handled the administrative end of the business, as we didn't have computers back then, at least none to speak of. She had to actually *file* files, can you believe it?

And I kept on cold calling.

I hired a salesman from an ad we put in the newspaper, and then as we grew, I hired even more, including office staff from that first agency I had worked. By this time, many of my ex-colleagues had moved on to other offices, though I did grab a few from the old agency directly (all is fair in insurance and war, right?). I knew these people, liked them, they knew the business, and I knew they'd do a good job for me.

I also came to represent more carriers. In a personal lines–specialty agency like mine, being able to offer customers multiple choices is important. The more insurance companies I could represent, the widest possible multivaried rating propositions I had for my potential clients. And, of course, with each new company you come to sell for, you learn different approaches to the business. And on top of learning more and more about the insurance business each day, I learned how to be a better boss and to run my shop more efficiently—a pure case of learning by doing.

It would take me quite awhile, not a small amount of reading, and even some seminars to find my leadership style. In the early to mid-90s, my wife and I would make a swinging hot date night a run to the local Barnes and Nobles (yes, we were crazy kids, huh?), and there I took to Michael Gerber's business books. I read *The E-myth: Why Most Businesses Don't Work and What to Do About It* cover to cover and would even come to order his tape series (again, this was way before you went online to download something). Listening to the whole series sitting in my kitchen, I made so many notes I filled up two legal pads. I still have those pads and over the years have referred to them often.

Gerber talks about pushing for your vision, imagining what your business is going to look like when it's done growing, reaching to be as big as you want it to be. His books and tapes helped me stiffen my backbone, helped me define traction in my office, manage my finances better, and grow to become the leader I wanted to be. This was why, years later when I sold my agency to the bank, I felt like somebody had taken my baby away, like a surgical removal of an organ . . . albeit for more money than I had ever made at one time in my life. I had put my heart and soul into getting things the way I wanted and spent so much energy in becoming the best I could be through my work.

My agency also got lucky in our first few years in business in that the type of insurance I was selling suddenly became mandatory in Arizona. This happens from time to time in our business. Laws are passed, and you happen to be involved in the niche bracket your legislature now demands all its citizens have. Carriers ached to have us on board, especially a well-oiled brokerage like mine.

We sailed along rather nicely to the end of the decade. I was making good money at a job I loved, and I had twenty-two carriers and nine employees. The only real hiccup for me personally was my growing dread over Y2K. Yes, looking back now we all easily recognize how foolish any worry was over the end-of-the-century-bug (even Kim Kardashian can break the net!). But like a lot of people, I dreaded the system going to double 00s. I was convinced a big crash was coming for our computer programs across the board. Surely, I was and still am a techno geek, and my agency was on the forefront of technology, as I will elaborate on a later, but I was more than slightly overwhelmed by the question of what was going to happen come the new century.

I could never have predicted the big changes that were coming for me and how they had nothing to do with Y2K.

Chapter 2

Transferring Risk: A Brief History of Insurance

"All mankind is divided into three classes: those that are immovable, those that are movable, and those that move."
Benjamin Franklin

The insurance industry has a rich history. I was surprised myself to learn how far back it went and specifically how each facet of coverage came into existence. For the most part, cargo, property, death, accident, and medical treatment insurance came into being on the backs of the old "necessity is the mother of invention" axiom.

The first-known records of insurance of any kind date from several thousand years before the Christian era. Chinese merchants devised a system for protecting themselves from losses they might incur when transporting their cargo by ship. Knowing they could potentially come up against storms, pirates, or running a vessel across a rocky shoal or other untoward possibilities while at sea, these merchants spread their cargo among the several ships of merchants looking to spread/protect their product in the same way. The prevailing school of thought here was that whatever could sink or destroy one ship one day would probably not destroy a whole fleet sailing across the sea for

25

several days. This grouping of sea merchant interests illustrates the basic tenet of our business: risk sharing. In this case, the merchants spread their risk by literally spreading their wares among a grouping of people with the same interest. Later on, of course, the model of our modern-day insurance business would grow into transferring risk to someone else and then paying them to incur this risk with the proviso that this person you pay will indeed pay you if the risk proves real and you incur some damage. But all this was years down the road from what the Chinese managed way back when.

In the historical Code of Hammurabi existed a provision for merchants who received a loan to fund their shipment. The person who took the loan would pay his money lender additional monies for the lender's guarantee to cancel their loan should the merchant's shipment be stolen or lost at sea. And in Rhodes, a general average was established so groups of merchants—like the aforementioned Chinese merchants—could insure their goods all together in a collected premium; goods were often jettisoned or lost in sinkage at this early stage of sea transport, as they were in China.

As stated before, necessity was surely the mamma of invention for ancient people.

The origins of life insurance seem to date back to early Greek and Roman civilizations. "Benevolent societies," or guilds, came to care for the families of their members who died. These groups would pay for funerals and cover household expenses, all from monies collected for this purpose, "insuring" the future care of members' families. These types of guilds had been in existence in one form or another since the Middle Ages, performing the same function. Later on, this idea would morph into the modern-day equivalent ("modern day" seventeenth century, that is) of "friendly societies," groups that would donate money collected from their members for any of their other members to use when undergoing an emergency.

Until the fourteenth century, it seems insurance policies were usually bundled with loans and other kinds of contracts. But in Genoa, in 1347, the first known contract only for insurance was enacted. Thus began the era of the insurance contract, allowing for insurance to be considered on its own, separate from loans or investments. To be sure, a big step as far as sellers of insurance are concerned. This most important piece of our business history proved especially useful initially in marine insurance.

Pedro de Santarém's *On Insurance and Merchants' Bets* was published in 1552. It is considered the first book printed on the sole subject of insurance.

Centuries later, in the 1600s, British merchants and ship owners began meeting at a coffee house named Lloyd's near the London docks. That name sounds familiar, right? In these furtive meetings, merchants and ship owners entered into agreements to share the profits of their voyages, as well as their possible losses (akin to the Chinese model). Some individuals were more willing than others to risk possibly hazardous trading voyages, and they'd come to underwrite the trips, becoming known as "underwriters." These individuals were the forerunners of the famous international insurance association Lloyd's of London, whose modern-day underwriters infamously now insure almost anything, from Betty Grable's legs for a cool $1 million, to the successful launch of a communications satellite.

Although the first insurance from Lloyd's was devised for ships' cargo—one could say business insurance truly started with sea trade—merchants began to band together to share other kinds of risk, including that of fire. In 1667, the first insurance company was founded the year after the Great Fire of London that destroyed thirteen thousand homes and left one hundred thousand people homeless. Thus property insurance was born.

The city of London also seems to be the originator of life insurance. The Amicable Society for a Perpetual Assurance Office, begun in the first few years of the 1700s, offered their members a life insurance plan with a fixed annual payment per share for members between the ages of twelve and fifty-five. At the end of each year this "amicable contribution" was divided between the wives and children of members who had died, in proportion, of course, to how many shares the heirs of the deceased happened to own.

As with sea travel prompting merchants to look for protection (insurance) of their goods, in the late 1800s, railroad travel became popular, and travelers on trains were looking for insurance . . . to protect their lives. Much in the mold of what would become our present disability insurance, the policies created by the Passengers Assurance Company, begun in 1848 in England, insured policyholders against the increasing number of deaths happening on the railroads of the day.

Train travel was certainly dangerous way back when it first began, but the people who needed to get to and fro in this manner were at least going to be insured.

In the "New World" of America, the first insurance company was founded by an association of store owners in 1735 to share the risk of fire destroying their wooden buildings; once again we see commerce leading the way when it comes to insurance. This association existed for a mere half decade, but none other than Benjamin Franklin soon founded the Philadelphia Contributionship for the Insurance of Houses from Loss by Fire in 1752. This company still exists—now named The Insurance Company of North America—and is still based in Philadelphia. Similar groups formed and split into various companies. Many—Hartford Fire Insurance Company, Aetna Life and Casualty Company, and the Travelers Insurance companies—came to be based in Hartford, Conn., labeling that New England city "The Insurance Capital of the United States."

As these companies grew and began seeing the need for risk sharing, they began to offer different kinds of insurance to more areas of the country. Since underwriters could not travel around the country on horseback to meet with all the people who might be interested in buying insurance—we've already seen how dangerous train travel was!—they began appointing agents to offer their insurance and accept premium contributions on their behalf. These agents were the first insurance salesmen.

This was the birth of the insurance agency system as we know it today in the U.S. As we see, and as I came to learn, much to my surprise, the business we are in had its start deep in human cultural history. Our industry has been a pillar of commerce and livelihood for people around the globe.

Chapter 3

Selling: The Old vs. the New

"The price of anything is the amount of life you exchange for it."
Henry David Thoreau, philosopher

The thought of selling my agency never occurred to me. I was in business for eight years, doing well, thirty-three years old with a great marriage, a couple of kids, and pretty much loving life. I loved being a niche agency. We would come to specialize in vehicle insurance, covering motorcycles, boats, cars, etc. Other than the century change computer quandary in the back of my mind, life couldn't have been better.

But man, would life change . . .

A few years before, I had been engaged in a joint venture with five regional banks. They were looking to invest in starting an insurance agency collectively. The insurance organization that I was part of at that time (as a volunteer board member) was instrumental in this early stage "insurance in banks" model. The group was made up of ninety-five professional insurance agents, mostly men in their forties—ancient guys to me as a twenty-three-year-old. They allowed me in to sit on the board, priding themselves in the magnanimous glow they felt showing the young punk how it was done, and I was grateful for the tutelage.

My interest in technology went hand in hand in building my agency. At our earliest stages, my company came to be known as a leader in the burgeoning tech scene, specifically how it related to the insurance business (the "older" brokers were fascinated by stuff as simple as how I could fax from my laptop). The group servicing the banks knew of my IT savvy as much as anything else, and may have wanted me around for my smarts in this area more than anything else . . . which was fine with me. I soaked up all I could about how to deal with banks during my time with that group: came to see how endless paperwork and contracts were pored over by bank attorneys; how one meeting begot another and another; learned "bank speak," that particular painfully methodical way of peppering what you say with big words to impress a crowd and make sure everyone is hanging on your laboriously long pauses.

Helping those banks and learning about all those processes would not only prove an invaluable education, but this work would change my life. Years after volunteering on that insurance board, a large mortgage company got ahold of me when they were looking to diversify. My reputation was such that I was the agency the bank approached—approached to buy!

When that bank first called, I had no idea what they had in mind. In fact, I didn't even take their first call, figuring they were just throwing out feelers. Considering what I had done regarding banks before, it seemed logical that they might be looking for a consultant or might be wanting me, yet again, for volunteer work. But by that point I was much too busy for that, and frankly, I felt I had moved on from what I had learned.

But no, these big guys were looking to buy.

You need to take yourself back to the mid-90s here, a boom time, with homeowners using their houses as ATMs, and mortgage banks wanting to gobble up businesses. Days later we received a second call from the bank, and again I ignored it. The "third time was the charm," though. Still not sure why the bank was calling, I agreed to meet some of their higher-level execs in the most impressive high-rise in the city, the Williams Center, to see why they were so actively pursuing little old me.

At that meeting, where I was undoubtedly impressed by my surroundings (heck, I ran a street-level shop, and these guys were playing in the red-carpet, wood-panel-wall big leagues), I was told that the bank wanted to buy my agency.

I was sent to go away and think of a price.

Man, talk about being thrown a curve ball! The last thing I thought I'd ever talk to these bank executives about was them wanting to buy my insurance agency. I was gob smacked over their offer—well, their offer of an offer; there was nothing definite on the table, and no money had been discussed. I mean, I knew I loved my agency, but here was somebody else, a big-time somebody else, showing the love by wanting to buy me. Yes, I had a solid reputation. I knew what I was doing and what's more I had a passion for doing it, which always makes something that much more attractive to those looking in at you. But I had never imagined selling what I was so into, what I jumped out of bed every morning aching to get to do, what fed, clothed, and gave my family a pretty great life. Suddenly, I had to think of this business I so loved, that I had built over a chunk of time, as a commodity.

I could go from agency owner to agency *seller* if indeed I wanted to. A world of possibility—not to mention a sudden influx of lots of cash—was being dangled before me. My work, always one of the defining factors of my life, was being validated in a way I had never considered. I remember even saying aloud, "How can I come to the right price here? I've given eight years of my life to this; it's my professional reason for being. How do I put a price on that?"

Now, remember the world way back then. Google had yet to be fully developed; the Internet was still in its infancy. The only real place for me to go to do any research on this problem—and yes, I know, what a problem to have, right, somebody wanted to give me money and buy my business!—was to consult my insurance industry trade journals. I was the kind of guy who put insurance magazines and trade journals aside until I could get to them during a long coffee break or maybe some weekend when there wasn't anything pressing with the family. These days people set aside whole weekends to catch up on a Netflix series; I "binge read" those journals hoping to get a clue how to value and price my agency.

I relied on the old model of how to sell, a traditional way of looking at all this, as much art as science. That's all I had to go on to assess the value of my shop and what those magazines and trade journals were advising.

The value of an agency is typically assessed from that agency's income, market, and assets. Makes sense, right? First, a potential buyer looks at how much the agency is making via commission presently and what they could make in the future through renewals. Second, they delve deep into the present marketplace of the insurance business, as much as the "market" the selling agency deals with—what carriers they use and what kind of insurance they sell. And last, a buyer takes a good, hard look at what the agency has in assets—if they have them—and even the actual components in their office, such as furniture, computers, etc. Yes, the assessment is a little more complicated than this, and I'll get into the nuts and bolts of it more specifically in what follows. But certain historical traditions have been considered—or at least were when I sold—ever since the beginning of the insurance business; another reason to know our history well.

So, off I went to do my due diligence—and that's a term I will come to use often here—to come to a price for what I thought my agency was worth.

The "Old Way"

The historic industry standard for pricing an agency comes down to considering an agency's revenue (its book) and offering 1.5 to 2x that revenue. If you own a captive agency—are representing "big boy" carriers with high brand recognition—this typically brings your shop to the higher end of the revenue scale. Especially in the older way of looking at things, the independent agency is typically valued lower than a captive one, but you will come to see later how my more "advanced" model of assessment often plucks out the positives of being an independent agency. I am not saying this out of conceit, but simply as a matter of fact. I often tell people who come to sell their agency to hold their hoped-for price close to their chest, as after a deep dive from me they might be surprised my offer is higher than the price they were thinking of asking.

I typically build on this older model and come to take my dive from considering an agency's EBITDA—earnings before interest, taxes, depreciation, and amortization—first and foremost. I will explore this more in chapter 5. Overall, numbers were pretty high a decade or so ago; agencies were selling high indeed when banks were grabbing up anybody and everybody. But that bubble has burst. I have run up against plenty of men and women who assume their agency is worth a lot more than it is because of the price their buddy sold at . . . decades ago. The market, which is something else measured in the old model—where your agency sits in the insurance marketplace specifically—is simply not as strong as it once was. Yes, the world and for our purposes, the U.S. economy, has gone through some startling economic upheavals in the past few decades, and that which affects commerce and finances affects the insurance business to be sure.

Weighed against the above, and as salient in the old way as in the new, is whether an agency has any liabilities and how big they might be. This is no small point as you will come to see, as this negative has tripped me not once, but twice, during my time buying agencies. I'm not even suggesting that the buyer is trying to slip something by me (most of the time) but liens, debts, and other hindrances, especially those that have been with you for a long time, often get forgotten simply because these are things you *want to* forget.

An agency's assets beyond its biggest asset, its book, include its office furniture and cash or sometimes stocks. While stocks can be quite lucrative—and I have done pure stock deals, though I don't like to, as you will see later—that "stuff" inside your four walls usually won't amount to such a significant number. Even if you happen to have twenty people occupying individual stations sitting on ergonomic chairs fronting ornately carved oak desks supporting the latest computers, these "things" won't represent all that big of a price tag when compared to the numbers calculated from checking an EBITDA and your book.

It really does come down to revenue and renewal rates within the niche you are working.

Making Your Agency More Valuable

Let's assume that when you're approached to sell, you've had time to take stock and consider your options. As I will strongly advise throughout every step of the way here, we will take it on faith that you have amassed a good team of experts and that you are weighing your options through dogged and determined research.

Yes, this is a big moment, so correctly weigh its significance. You will come to see the insurance business in a way you have yet to. Look at your agency beyond what client of yours is presently up for renewal or what carrier you might have to presently massage. For the first time, like when the bank asked me to go home and think of a price for my shop, you will now come to consider how much someone else values your baby, the child you created and coddled for years at great sacrifice.

Walking into any further negotiations for your agency without having a price in mind for what you feel your agency is worth will set you in a defensive position immediately. Buyers pounce on this kind of wishy-washy ineptitude. I have seen them circle a potential seller like vultures for any perceived weakness in a sale. Lots of times the people you come up against wanting to buy your agency have done lots of buying before, like I have. If this is your first time selling—which most likely it is if you are reading this book—it behooves you to at least walk into the process with as strong a hand as possible; if you do not have the experience of selling on your side, at least have a concrete price in mind. Doing so is your first and best defense against getting ripped off in a sale.

Now I showed you above how one goes about the historic way of setting a price, and in the buying chapter (chapter 5), I will show how I come to my price above and beyond the historic model. But what should be more important to you, even before you come to a price, is how you can increase the value of your agency. How does one paint lipstick on the proverbial prized pig? No, no. I'm not calling your agency a pig—you know how much I love insurance, how valuable I think we all are. But you do have to consider gussying things up if you are going to sell for the best price. Certain things you might not be able to change—your capital might be restricted, you might have more pressing concerns to attend to, cleaning up some back taxes you might owe to the I.R.S. comes to mind here—but if you can make the changes I suggest, do so.

Being proactive at the outset speaks to an important point in this process: the second you get an itch to sell, the moment you feel there might be a possibility you want to, even if you don't put your agency on the market for two years, get into selling mode. Plenty of business instructional manuals advise owners to be thinking about selling the second they start a business. I don't subscribe to this way of doing things; that's too much of a fatalistic mindset for me. But on the other side of the coin, I have seen time and time again, as an agency owner slowly loses his or her interest in the business for whatever reason, they can let a lot slide by them. It's simply human nature that the less passion you have for something, the less you will devote your time and energy to it. Time is the enemy here as profits begin to slip, sales growth stalls, and new clients are not acquired.

Snap decisions will not serve you well when selling. Rushing to get out, hastily planning your exit will force your hand and never prove the most fruitful. But if you wait too long simply stagnating, you will bleed the value from your agency as well.

As I say, some of the changes and proactive measures I mention next might not be possible given the size of your receivables or other factors that could hinder you, but plenty of these will be available if you allow the time for them. What you are looking to do here is to make that which you have to sell—and everything reflects back to how valuable your book is—a commodity a whole bunch of buyers can't ignore. And believe me, having multiple buyers interested in you works well in your favor. Just like you'd slap some paint on that house you are selling, maybe bring your car in for its last tune-up before slipping a FOR SALE sign in the window, you do want to take care to make your agency the best it can be so you can get the most money for it.

How does one do this?

Embrace Digital

As a leader in the intersection of technology and the insurance business, RIGHTSURE brings quite a bit of the digital to bear when buying an agency. The facts, figures, and data I scribbled across pieces of paper down at the coffee shop years ago are now the basis for the digitized computer programs we implement facts and figures into for our buying. A couple of years back I spent a Memorial Day weekend digitizing everything in my life, from important family papers, kids' coloring books, letters from my wife, and of course EVERY SINGLE DEAL OR TRANSACTION I ever engaged in. OK, so maybe I am a junkie for this kind of stuff, but the point is, modern-day technology relates to you, the seller, when it comes to increasing the valuing your company. Believe me; it is not just from my point of view that I advise you to modernize.

Selling insurance is not unlike selling ice cream (and yes, insurance is more delicious) in that we are delivering a product. And even better than ice cream, most people come to need insurance in one way or another. Our ice cream is not ours; it's made outside our shop, from our carriers, and it's not much different than the ice cream our customers, the insured, will find at any other shop/agency. You can get a variety of flavors, sprinkles on your cone, even double scoops. But what makes our customers come back for our sweet treats time and again (renew or buy different/more insurance from us) is how we deliver our product, how we present a nice clean countertop, and spin out cones and cups speedier than that shop down the street.

We use technology to give our customers the best ice cream buying experience.

I was a big proponent early on, as I have already related, of learning all I could about all that was happening around me, as much for my business as for my education. I took to every new development coming down the pike. I loved getting my hands dirty and seeing what could be used, what was a flash-in-the-pan or what I could "MacGyver" in making something work for me. It took a lot of trial and error. I won't kid you. In fact, even nearly thirty years in the business I am vetting new metrics and bigger, better, faster ways of doing things every day. We constantly challenge the technology to make sure it consistently makes our customers' experience the best it can be. We are learning all the time, and failing as much as succeeding.

I look at RIGHTSURE as foremost a technology company that excels at mining policyholder data, followed by a marketing firm whose product just happens to be the greatest product the world has ever known, insurance. This doesn't make me any less an insurance guy. My love for selling insurance has never lessened. But the way we sell it now is informed by the technology we use to better our policyholders' dealings with us. I like to think of us as daily challenging the old way of doing things, even if the old way means how it was done a week ago.

You don't have to get all caught up in algorithms or software to understand the simple progression of things here, for our business or any other. Remember the insurance history chapter? By the time agents came on the scene, they were going out to find customers on foot and by horseback, then by train when it became available, then soon it was by car, and after that, by phone. These days we "go out" via email or Skype; it's all just a progression that follows technology. But a pleasant and engaging voice on the other end of the phone, or even some face time with a client, also pays dividends, and we still deliver in this way. But we use the tools available to create an ever better customer experience.

But as I have learned time and time again, you may have access to the better mousetrap, but if you don't know how to use that mousetrap or, more importantly, how to use it to catch the kind of mouse you are after, the mousetrap is just another mousetrap. In fact, leave off the mouse part. If what you are using doesn't end up working for you in the end, it could turn out to be a trap for you in general.

Anyone with a checkbook can go out and buy any third-party technology or an Apple computer. For little outlay of money, even the smallest-sized office can set up a telephone management system, be it voice mail or call forwarding. And with only a small amount of time you can rifle through a few YouTube tutorials and learn a whole bunch about online marketing. If you want to get specific, there are a whole bunch of wonderfully efficient insurance computer software programs that will do lots of the work for you; every day there's a new one coming on the market. I am constantly amazed at what new stuff programmers think up. But unless you know how to use what you are buying, or more precisely, how to apply it to your specific needs, well, enjoy looking at that mousetrap because it won't be catching mice for you.

What makes us different and what I have worked hard on, regarding technology and this business, is RIGHTSURE's technology "stack." Over time—and again lots of trial and error and not a small amount of money spent—we have acquired and built the technology we use to not only work but work synergistically in all of what we do, right down the line, stacked in our business.

Let me give you an example from one of the most-used systems in our office; I dare say, it's probably one of your most-used systems as well.

Our phone system receives thousands of calls weekly. But we have set up the system, bringing another program in on top (stacking) to make sure the calls coming in are distributed equally among my agents. On top of this, I didn't want customers leaving voice mails or having to deal with that "Press 1 for . . . Press 2 for . . ." demoralizing automated system. So, we have an integrated cue system that keeps our clients on the line for as short a time as possible. A recording assures them that the next available agent will take their call as fast as possible, which my agents will do because of this cuing system, and kindly thanks our caller for their patience.

Time is precious here. In fact, around my offices, we are maniacal about speed. I always think of *Rocky 11* where Mickey tells Rocky, "Speed's what we need; we need greasy, fast speed!" The core of our data mining is to make sure our agents answer and respond to calls quicker than any other agency. I am well aware you can go online and with a few clicks of your mouse spin up a quote. I know that with the advent of TV insurance ads featuring "Flo" and little green talking geckos, people can make a quick phone call and never need endure being kept on hold from a phone agent.

Furthermore, and with even more technology stacking, when someone calls RIGHTSURE, if they are already in our system, we have the program in place for our computers to match that phone number with the caller's file. When our agent comes on the phone to talk with this client, the client information comes up immediately with no lag time, no stuttering around who the caller might be. I know plenty of agencies who still use paper files, files someone has to go and retrieve when sitting on a call. This doesn't work for us. Further, if one of our clients were to buy a new boat or a motorcycle—something they would need insurance on sooner or later—they can take a picture of it, upload to their policy file via email, and send it to us so we can include it in their file.

This is just one example of how we stack and use technology to make the customer experience better and, in the end, possibly increase our profits.

It all comes down to how best to measure psychographics— our consumers'/insureds' attitudes, values, lifestyle, etc.—with demographics—those same consumers'/insureds' gender, age, income, education levels, etc. This is that part of the multilayered RIGHTSURE equation where we first mine policyholder data (or look to gain this information for potential new policyholders) then use it ("market" it) for our purposes to best determine who is buying our product and why.

The who and why applies to the property and casualty insurance we specialize in with renters, house buyers, students, vehicle owners, men, and women all the way down the line. Once we answer the "who" and the "why," we can go out and find the best places to advertise. We see renters seeking insurance or parents wanting insurance for their child moving into a college dorm for the first time, so we make our presence known by advertising in apartment rental journals or college literature.

Asking who and why, we found that first-time homeowners often buy the whole kit and caboodle of coverage from the bank or lending institution giving them their mortgage. Usually, as overwhelmed as these first-time homeowners are with the daunting task of buying their first property, they welcome bundling everything they come to need with one company. Acquiring this knowledge, we made many joint ventures with banks and credit unions after measuring the psychographics with demographics using the most up-to-date software.

With our current clients, we use our technology for consistent deep data mining, arriving at logical assumptions we can use to sell. For instance, a single woman or man between the ages of thirty and thirty-five who only has auto with us might need renter's insurance, when one considers their psychographics with demographics. Then again, maybe this person is a homeowner; we have a bunch of insurances we can offer in this regard. Conversely, a man or woman at forty years old might have acquired a bit more toys; maybe they need a motorcycle or boat insured. We make sure to send out text alerts, email updates, and postcard prompts that will interest each of these people, reminding them that not only can we cover what is presently important to their lives, but the more we cover for them, the more of a possible discount we can offer.

And all of this is measured, dissected, and acted on—mined if you will—using the technology we do.

So, I do know of what I speak when I advise . . .

First and foremost, **digitize ALL your client files**. The prospect of looking through reams and reams of paper, poring over your book in this way, is woefully unattractive to the modern-day buyer—not only to me—and I dare say you could lose a sale if you are not prepared in this most basic of ways. You'll want to begin the process of digitizing your agency's information the second you get an inkling that you might be in the market to sell. Yes, it can be a giant time suck, but this step, as off-putting and costly as it might be initially, will make your agency more valuable at the time of sale than you can imagine.

Technology also plays into **firming up your EFT or electronic funds clients**. You don't need me to tell you how advantageous it is to get your clients on electronic billing. You can save your insured around $20 a month each when you don't have to bother with paper statements and mailings: you don't have to chase people down for payments; you can take retention temperature much easier when you have people on EFT. I can emphatically state that the more clients you have signed on via electronic billing at the time of your sale, the more attractive your agency will be and therefore the more you can get for it.

Another case for digitization is that **it is easier to consolidate your insureds among your highest compensation carriers\markets.** Incentives are in place from many insurance companies to bring clients over . . . you know this already; I'm not telling you anything new. But if you have your records digitized, monitoring these clients via EFT, you can get these clients over to agencies that will offer you discounts and incentives, many of which you can pass on to the customer.

Vet your buyer. I will get into this in detail in a bit, but suffice it to say if you are selling internally to an officer or some other personnel of your agency, you should already have plenty of intelligence on this buyer. Selling to this type of a buyer is delicate, though, as it goes against one of my tried and true rules a seller should abide by: let as few people as you can know you are selling. Selling internally, the cat is out of the bag. But for our purposes here, we have been and will continue to assume that you are selling to someone externally. And if you are indeed doing so, **the best way to learn about someone these days is via the Internet.**

For many people of a certain generation, the digital world has passed them by, as its infiltration might be one of the reasons these people might want to get out of the business. Heck, I know about this digital stuff, work with it daily, and it's often an uphill climb for me to keep up! I appreciate agency owners as much not having the time to work their business anymore as much as feeling they are not of these modern times, feeling they are wading in the sour end of how business is now being done. I know it rattles the brain even to consider some of what technology now offers, especially when you did not grow up with this technology and rely on younger employees to see you through the deep waters. But I must reiterate that when selling, embrace technology best you can by digitizing ALL your client files, firming up your EFT or electronic funds clients, consolidating your insureds among your highest compensation carriers\markets, and vetting your seller.

You will come to see later the steps that RIGHTSURE has to go through post acquisition and how inefficient paper documents are to us as we execute deep dives to contact your carriers, which will become our carriers after the sale, and your clients, who are ours now to take care of and monitor and to make sure monies are flowing to where they should.

Get All Your Financials in Order
Start cleaning up your financials, especially trust and operating accounts, company payables, loans, and notes. Start reining in discretionary expenses and identify outside subproducing business not owned by your agency. If you have any tax quandaries sticking out there, even little ones, get these settled as well. It could take awhile from the time you put your agency up for sale to the actual time of the sale; you will want to keep your financials as clean and as transparent

as possible during this time to engender confidence in the buyers coming to consider you.

Dollar amounts can get mighty big when selling. You are going to start seeing numbers you may never have dealt with before. Deals might be presented that you have never considered or even thought possible. For your sale to go as smoothly as you like (and smoothly=lucratively), your financials need to be in tip-top shape. No buyer wants to encounter debts or financial impropriety you never saw coming or were simply trying to ignore.

Which leads to . . .

Hire Experts

You know how this goes, the second you start having trouble with your knee and tell a few friends about the pain, suddenly everybody you know is an orthopedist. The same is true when you begin floating the idea of selling your agency. Well-intentioned advice though it may be, sometimes even coming from reputable sources—other agency owners, family members who run a business, employees even—you should really only take business advice about selling your agency from people who know about selling, or more specifically, the people you hire to help you in your selling.

I cannot advise too strongly, and I will hammer home this point: **Have a good CPA and business attorney on retainer for your upcoming sale.** You will need competent, trustworthy advice in the art of the deal, regardless of what kind of deal you come to make. Especially if you have never sold an agency before—and few people go down this road more than once—you need to present a united front that buyers will take seriously.

Your team, be they attorney, secretary, business advisor, even mentor (or all of the above) should insulate you—but not isolate you—from the details you need not worry about. They should help in vetting buyers, figuring exactly what are your deal breakers and what points can be negotiated. They should work to get you off of concepts that are simply not valid or convince you to reconsider terms that they know are simply not possible with what you have to offer. You are going to pitch your buyers a price sooner more than later, but you shouldn't be pitching your team. With them, you will need an honest and sometimes painful reality check so you come to a balance between what you want for your agency and what its true value is. You are too close to the situation. This is your baby; you have an emotional investment. But emotion will not serve you well in structuring and executing your deal. What your experts might present to you could even go against many of your preconceived notions.

Consider that, as a buyer I am much more confident in the agency I am about to buy if they have a well-informed, knowledgeable team around them. Professionals who know as much or more than me make the process go faster and at times can present some deep dive idea I've yet to consider. I'm not intimidated. On the contrary, I am thrilled when dealing with a cracker-jack group who wants to see the sale go through smoothly and fast. When I present my assessment and throw out my numbers, people in the know understand where I am getting my facts and figures. We might not always agree—negotiation is another art of the deal—but at least when we all speak the same language it makes for better understanding. Maybe I am the rare case in that I am not looking to get over on you; I'm not prepared to slip in some fancy footwork you won't catch, hoping to sneak maximum profit from the acquisition at your expense. Sorry, I am too honest for that. I want the experts of your team to work with my expert team in arriving at the best deal for us both. Quite frankly that's good business, as far as I'm concerned, and I have a reputation to uphold.

In the end, you hire the experts you do as much to steer you through the legalities of the deal as to get you close to what you want.

Vetting Buyers

Use the net to aid you in vetting buyers, but remember, not all buyers are right for all agencies.

As I will elaborate on later, I am only interested in buying specific brokers selling for under a certain amount and selling only a specific kind of insurance. We often hear the word "discriminate" used negatively, but I discriminate in who I want to be in business with, what agencies I want to buy, how much the agency makes, what carriers they sell for, and what kind of an agency they are. This vetting from my end, even before I will consider a deal, has well served my company and the agencies we come to buy again and again.

As the seller, you can be just as discriminating, and in fact, it behooves you to be. I suggest you start looking for a buyer that has the interests of your clients in mind. Some acquisition firms are only interested in gobbling up acquisitions on top of acquisitions, looking to satisfy a minimum buyout that's required by the investors loaning them money. Other firms are looking for strategic fits. I am not saying these buyers won't offer you a fair market price, but they may not be so inclined to go the extra mile to do the deep dive (more on this later). They tend to see the agencies they acquire in a big grouping and less as individual brokers with specific clientele needing equally individual handling. Buyers with the deepest pockets might not be the best ones to sell to, as you will come to learn from cautionary reports and other agency owners' reviews.

And if a buyer does not know your niche well when figuring your worth, they may not know how to explore the nuances that make your agency worth more in your specific niche.

An agency that operates in your current vertical or is interested in starting in your vertical could be a good buyer. But check well to make sure that this agency cultivates a climate that will embrace your clients and staff or at least is aware that a bad culture fit will destroy all that you have built over the years. Simply put, **is the buyer you are considering empathetic to understanding your processes, your clients, and your philosophy of business?**

Sellers tell me that they chose us because they believed we were empathetic to what they had built. As they deal with us, they become convinced that we will be careful in the handoff for every single client that we will become entrusted with. Especially with smaller agencies, a personal connection with clients is one that is often deeply cultivated. While it is true that sellers want the most they can get for their agency, they also often want to sell to someone who has an interest in continuing the legacy they have built.

I'm often surprised how many buyers don't understand the above, or how they come to see this as simply a touchy-feely concern from the seller's point of view. But many a buyer gets bitten on their you-know-what failing to consider this salient insurance truth: **If the buyer doesn't seem to have the best interest of an agency's clients in mind and won't continue in a particular broker's legacy and ways of service, those clients that used to be loyal to the agency will not be loyal to the new unsympathetic buyer of that agency, and will jump ship as soon as they can.**

Besides using the net, ask around within your community and specific niche about the buyer coming to your table. These days a buyer can come from anyplace, even one not directly related to insurance. When I sold, the bank that bought me was just starting to delve into buying insurance brokerages; this didn't make them a bad buyer, though. Buyers are likely to be other insurance agencies, but where a buyer may not have the specific knowledge of selling insurance, they might be hungry enough to bolster your reputation and take your agency into the future quite swimmingly.

Clean Up That Partnership

If you have a partner in your business, make sure they are on the same page as you . . . or try to get them close. Nothing can be more frustrating than having an equity owner that's been by your side for many years and is now holding up the sale of the business. You may be ready to head to the links or spend more time with your grandchildren, but what if your partner does not have the same goals in mind? Unfortunately, in my experience of buying an agency from partners—something I have done only a few times in my acquisition career—even agreeing on the smallest details of a deal can prove most problematic for some owners. I am sorry to report that by the time most partners come to the table to sell, one of the main reasons they both want to get out is that they can't much stand one another any longer. And these negative feelings may make the sale difficult indeed.

What's the solution if your agency happens to be in a less than friendly partnership? How might you facilitate an easier sale or come to a unified front to present to your seller? I suggest—as I will suggest all throughout this book—to keep emotions out of the process. Yes, I know this is hard, especially in a situation where you and your partner have grown to hate even the sight of one another. But for the good of the sale (which really means the highest amount you can get from your buyer), you need to take all those decade-long resentments and personal differences, put them away for a later date (and therapist), and indeed solidify your purpose as that classic unified front. If the two of you even need to hire separate attorneys—and this is something I would certainly advise—as much to figure your agency's sale price as to keep you principals from throwing down at board meetings, do so as fast as you can.

Can disgruntled partners queer a sale? Need I answer? This is why, given my druthers, I'll always prefer buying an agency that is solely owned, only ever having to deal with one guy or gal (with their team of experts in place) making the final decisions. It makes my future integration that much easier. I don't instantly run away from a partnership, but these kinds of sales can be much harder to execute. And I won't even begin to tell you the things I have found out about one partner over another that the partners don't know about or reveal until I come back with my deep dive!

If you are part of a partnership, I say to both of you, come to an agreement and get your ducks in a row before you come to me.

Determining Your Terms: What It Is You Want to Sell and How You Are Selling It

I have seen a plethora of possibilities presented when an agency comes to sell. No two deals are alike, and researching specifics from one agency sale to another could make your head spin. This is why, while I advise that you do indeed get those pros in to work your deal, in the end, only you, the seller, will know exactly how you will structure your sale: the terms, what it is you are selling, and how you are selling it.

One of the concerns that determines the type of sale you will undergo—what you are looking to sell of your agency, if not all of it—is how much you, the seller, still want to have a hand in things. I have as much seen people want to get out lock, stock, and barrel, be done with their agency in a fast, clean sweep as I have seen plenty of people who want to ease out in a long transition where they stay in selling. I certainly can't advise you as to which will work for you—there are advantages and disadvantages to all approaches, and sometimes they don't become apparent until well after the sale—but I do advise weighing your options best you can on all accounts.

Again, use your experts as a sounding board. You have hired them to see the forest for the trees for you.

Another factor in determining the terms of the deal is how best to minimize taxes. Rest assured, coming from the buyer end of things, I am concerned with this piece of the deal as much as you, and I'm sympathetic to a situation where we can lessen the hit we are both going to take. Again, here is where your CPA will come in and help you crunch the numbers. More on taxes later, I promise.

Last, and probably the biggest factor in determining both what you sell and how you sell it is, bluntly put, **how much cash you need right now**. Sure, taxes come to play here, but I have bought from folks who needed a big influx of money ASAP (read on about my second nightmare deal) as well as from folks who had their finances structured in such a way that they are paid over time. And remember, cash is not the only currency in deals. Stock options and other lucrative bon mots also make a sale.

The creative ways of structuring deals are multitudinous, and the terms you will come to should always work in your favor. Explore these well, pore over your options with your experts, and get as creative as you like. This is your deal and you have to live with it, so make it the best it can be for your needs. As hard as it was for me that first time selling (remember me full fetal back at the Del Coronado?), I made a deal I could live with—and live very well indeed—after the initial smoke cleared for me that I was no longer the owner of my agency.

You need to be able to live with your sale.

To Specialize or Not to Specialize; That Might Be the Question
Like consolidation, specializing can be a positive, proactive measure
to increase your agency's price tag. This could be a rather drastic step,
but one not without risk. And many agencies simply can't implement
specialization or have no care to do so. But for a niche agency adding
another specialty or the shop that has the time and resources to
implement changes or additions to their focus, many buyers will see
specialization as increasing an agency's value.

Surely specialization narrows the market for those buyers who
might come a calling—one of the risks mentioned above—but consider
both the buyer who may be looking to acquire a niche agency or one
looking to branch out from what they do presently. Or think about
how valuable you will look to plenty of brokers out there building
their brand from your specialty.

Last, in many cases, specializing cuts out the excess baggage, the
veritable dead weight you maybe have been carrying around for a
long time, or it helps you cut your losses on types of insurance your
agency has simply never been good at selling. If executed early enough
(again, to get specialization up and running you'll need to implement
it years before you sell), you might see a considerable rise in profit,
making your book more valuable at the time of your sale.

Cutting Expenses=Downsizing
A buyer like me executing the four Ds in a deal—a **d**ue **d**iligent **d**eep
dive—will be able to see beyond your current financials and route
out potential you might not have been mining in recent years, simply

because you don't have the energy any longer to run your agency. But even if you don't come across a buyer as smart as me, you might still want to consider those expenses that are hemorrhaging money. And one of those biggest is employee salary.

Long-term employees earning a large salary because of seniority, or having too many employees aboard for a dwindling client load, will cause an imbalanced financial situation. The hard truth might be that trimming will be needed here before you even float the idea of selling your agency. I can most assuredly report that when a buyer comes to look at your most recent earnings, if he or she doesn't see some sort of an increase in profit, or in the worst scenario sees a flatlining of revenue over the past few years, your sale might be dead before it even begins.

As with specializing, simply jettisoning employees is not an easy fix. In fact, this might run completely against your ethos, so no one is going to blame you if you can't downsize. I know when I have to let people go, it burns me to the core! But again, if your financials are not showing strong or at least even, cutting expenses could prove smart for your sale.

Know, as Well as Accept, the Impediments for Your Potential Buyer

Yes, we are in the best business ever, aren't we? But it is not without its negatives. I'll own up to that, as much as you should when selling. You need to be realistic, as you hopefully have been when listening to your team about how much your agency might be worth in the current marketplace with the type of insurance you are selling.

As much as you will proudly come to terms with what makes your specific agency so valuable, you need to recognize that which does not. Beyond going digital, getting your financials in order, downsizing, etc., I also need to impress upon you to be realistic, and again, your team should be hammering this point home. Every business has its limitations, no matter how many clients you have, how high off your stationery the company logo is embossed, or how many likes you may have on Facebook.

Yes, I know you want to get out, but . . .

Buyer and seller are always going to be coming at the sale from two different mindsets. Sure, both parties have to meet on a price, but remember when selling, hard as this is for me to say, your buyer can't much care about your retirement when considering a price. Yes, he or she might be like me, interested in hearing of your plans, wanting to keep in touch via Facebook posts of the vistas you come to and the great times you are having. Maybe it's conceit on my part, but I do like to know that, in some small way, I might have been responsible for the seller's golden years. But when you are coming to price your agency, sifting through facts and EBITDA data with your team, your retirement should be subtext. Certainly, your looming European vacation or the grandkids' college funds figure into the overall plan here, but the amount you need for these things shouldn't influence the price you are asking for your agency. Only what your agency is worth is what should influence the price of your agency.

Further Consideration: What the Market Bears (and Bares)

I was being conservative when I mentioned that the marketplace isn't as healthy now as it was ten years ago. By all estimates—and something none of us wants to admit—the decline has been on us all for nearly thirty years. Yes, we have all heard the stories of guys and gals who retired well and never looked back, but things really "ain't what they used to be" in so much of the American marketplace.

But this history should not discourage you. The fact is that the axiom "Not all insurance agencies are comparable" could be chiseled into the Mount Rushmore of insurance, had we one. The marketplace fluctuates in specific ways that can certainly affect the price of what your agency is worth. Unfortunately, lots of these factors you can't do anything about. That's not to say, though, that you shouldn't be aware of them and use them in calculating your sale price.

Consider that hundreds of smaller insurance agencies are bought by larger ones all the time. These acquisitions as much whittle away the number of agencies out there as they drive industry-wide consolidation and oftentimes skew numbers. If you are using the market to gauge what your industry is worth but are not taking into account the rise in fair market value that comes from this consolidation—a simple supply and demand equation—then you are doing yourself a disservice. Surely, you need to take into consideration your geographic location, your state's laws that may be changing—or will never change—even a sudden influx of highly popular commercials altering the public to the kind of insurance you sell (thank God for funny female spokespersons, hummable tag lines, and green lizards). But the point is, even though most U.S. industry is not as full to the coffers as it was years ago, a little exploration of your specific marketplace, especially true for a niche agency, might reveal surprising results.

Buyer competition also drives price. Look around you. See what is happening with the buying and selling of agencies in your area as well as in your niche. Again, supply and demand come into play here. Quite often, by simply sticking around long enough, you might end up being the only game in town.

Keep Your Price Close to Your Chest
When I mentioned in the selling chapter that often we come back with a higher sale price than the seller comes to on his own, I wasn't kidding. I also wasn't kidding when I advised that it is best for you to keep the price you come to to yourself for as long as you can. In fact, if your buyers are coming in with higher bids than you imagined, you need never tell anyone that your own price was lower.

Demand Terms of the Deal Privacy
There is no need for any of the insurance carriers to know the details of your transaction; let them guess. In my dealings with buying agencies, we typically create a simple offer and acceptance letter that is mutually executed and notarized. Later we contact carriers with what they need to know when they need to know it. Our actual

Asset Purchase Agreement or Stock Purchase documents are not shared with anyone but the seller and our CPA, assuming there is no business broker involved on your end. Oh yes, people will inquire, and some carriers might even make you feel you are honor bound to divulge this information, but you are not and should not.

Also, it's a good idea to make sure potential buyers sign a preliminary confidentiality agreement, especially if you are entertaining multiple offers.

A Few Parting Shots

I should call this section "what I shouldn't tell you, but I am going to tell you anyway." I can't give you a full assessment of the buying and selling of insurance agencies without giving you some advice regarding what you should or should not do when you sit down with a potential buyer.

I always tried to conduct my business with the most honesty and transparency as I could, especially on the second go-around. I knew I had to march ever forward into the imploding world of finances with caution. People were more than slightly skittish after the banks failed, after mortgage rates sailed out of control, after the entire country ran for cover. How could I ever get someone signed up with me unless they trusted me? Yes, my religious background teaches a strict moral code, but it also made good business sense to me to keep things on the up and up as possible.

So here I am laying my cards out on the table. If you are thinking of selling and would consider me as a buyer, I want you to know you are not only getting someone sympathetic to your needs, but someone trustworthy (and I'm not lying about that!).

So, ready for some bean-spilling?

Chapter 4

RIGHTSURE: My Second Time at Bat

"People don't buy what you do. They buy why you do it."
Simon Sinek

No one could have predicted—or maybe it had been predicted and we were all just ignoring it—the crash that came to the banking world in 2008. If ever there was a feeling of having the rug pulled out from under your feet, man, that was it.

As I mentioned, I stayed on at the bank after I sold my agency. Part of my deal was that they would employ me for the next five years, and I grew with them during that time to make a very good salary. In no time at all I came to help the CEO and CFO in lucrative agency acquisitions. I was taking private chartered flights to destinations across the country, running the bank's insurance group and subsidiaries with two hundred employees under me. I felt I couldn't lose and, I hate to admit it, but if there was any time in my life that I wasn't acting like the most exemplary Jeff Arnold everybody knows and loves, it was then. I truly was drinking the corporate Kool-Aid, acting like a typical high-energy control freak. Hindsight is 20/20, of course. I don't much like "that" guy when I think about him now, but there I was living the dream and, more than I'd like to recall, being a class A jerk.

Sure, there were hiccups along the way; how could any big corporation not have them? Mainly, I found the bank's IT department lacking, to say the least. Coming to the bank as the techno guy I was, when it came to anything technical, I figured I could do what needed to be done. It was all I could do, even at the best of times, to get an IT guy off his butt to come to my office or execute minor tasks. I have never met a programmer or IT tech who said they couldn't do just about anything. But these guys who only ever answered YES to my requests at the bank, time and again executed the job so poorly or simply took so long to get it done that I was left exasperated by the delay. Yes, I know there are wonderful IT guys out there, but find a great IT guy who can execute well, and he will be irreplaceable. Once again, it was reiterated to me how good an idea it is to keep up on things in case you have to do them yourself.

But for the most part, my job was pretty good. I was in the money, humming along, building an acquired agency roster as well as a solid reputation as the guy who could get things done. So I can tell you that when the crash came, we were all schooled right quick. Suddenly, I was out of that seemingly all-perfect job. There was nothing left of the insurance operations; the bank was shutting its doors. Lights out, the fat lady was singing, the world as I knew it was no more.

I figured I'd get back into that which I knew best and had loved a lot. And really, what choice did I have? I needed to work as much to support my family and myself as to invest my life with purpose, to pursue that which I had been working hard for all this time. I began to put into place the deal that would have me buying back my old agency from my failing employer at double the price they had bought it from me, but it would be mine to do with as I pleased. I'd be back in the insurance business game, ready to stake my claim all over again.

Well, not quite. Another wonderful lesson in due diligence came my way when, after I bought my agency back, surfing a long process doing so, I was served with suit papers for a cool one billion dollars. Yes, it is a wild story, and I will tell you about it in a bit, but first, back to the implosion . . .

In the mess that was the national bank failure of 2008, I believe it was all of ten days from the time I was told of the crisis to when I officially lost my job. Things moved fast when the end finally came, an end we couldn't have imagined. I remember the moment exactly. At 5:01 p.m., my BlackBerry began ringing (remember BlackBerrys?), and upon answering my little portable device, I heard my CEO asking me to come over and see him. There were two miles between our offices, and although we were friends and saw one another often, I didn't frequently come to him. As I drove over, I thought, *Well, this is it. The bank may be engaged in cost cutting, or my constant battles with the IT department have made me not worth having around anymore; they are letting me go. It's been a good run, but my time is done.* But the real story was that the entire bank was done, the whole banking industry was in free fall.

When the CEO bid me into his office and I took the seat across from his desk, he simply said: "Well, Jeff, that's it, we are closing. Nothing you've done. It has been a real pleasure working with you."

I got back to the office around the time an inner office fax made the rounds, laying out the amazing situation the CEO had told me. Stupefied as my employees, we all switched on the TVs in our offices and watched history in the making, a history of which we were in the middle.

I came in for the next two months, unpaid, working to get my employees paid as we shut down completely. There was no plan in place for what was happening, no precedent for a nationwide banking fallout like this. Yes, there had been the Great Depression, and plenty of my coworkers were greatly depressed, but what did any of us know about a bank crash?

I didn't have anywhere else to go, and that's when I began working on the deal from within the bank to buy back my old insurance agency. Why the heck would they want it, I figured. Look what was happening between their four walls. If I could raise the cash, wouldn't they welcome selling my agency back to me and having some bucks in hand? Buying it back would not be easy, though.

Over the next few months, I'd be competing with other buyers, as well as facing the fact that few lenders out there were in a position to make loans. The nationwide bank failure was rocking the federal government and threatening to thrust the U.S. into socialism, so was it any wonder that few banks were ready to make a loan to a guy who had just worked for a bank and wanted to buy back his old insurance company that *that* bank presently owned?

I did have a bit of luck on my side, or more precisely, that "don't ever burn a bridge" axiom worked in my favor. A guy I had befriended in the banking community, somebody we had hired during our staff ramp-up, had left us to go work as a commercial loan officer in a huge bank in Tucson (smart guy getting out as he did when he did). This huge bank was one of the few doing OK, and when I told my buddy of my plan to buy back my agency, he told me that considering my reputation and knowing how serious I was, he could help me get some funding. I'd have to carry a heavy note—we took a second mortgage on our house to do so—and I wouldn't get the full amount I needed. Still, he assured me he could help me get a bulk of the money to buy the agency.

As I said, I had to compete with another buyer wanting my old agency, and I paid too much for it, really. But I did manage to buy my agency back by November of that year and with a substantial salary cut for God knew how long, I jumped back into selling insurance.

But, as I said, not without getting sued for one billion dollars. I think I can now tell that story without shaking in my boots.

I wasn't even in the office at the time and had only been back running my agency for two months. Imagine my surprise then when my secretary called to tell me that we had just been served by a court representative with a letter. I asked her to open it, and she replied that I was being sued for that cool billion. Of course, I hadn't done anything to warrant the suit. But I was caught up in all the drama that the industry was embroiled in. The trustee in their bankruptcy grabbed me in a big sweep from his own due diligence, faulty though it was, and served me.

What had happened was that when I took over ownership of my agency, I had asked the old IT department—yes, that very IT department I had always had friction with—to transfer the agency's insureds data over to me. This is the first big step any buyer executes after an acquisition. In fact, this information is crucial. How else would I get this information than asking for it through the usual channels? I simply asked my ex-employer, via email, for the files to be transferred. This should have been routine. But my inquiry, what I would come to call "that dreaded email," threw up a red flag for the trustee who was looking for any irregularities. Quite frankly, he was being overzealous in wanting to catch somebody doing something wrong in the bank's fallout. And guess who he found to pin his suspicions on?

This is an oversimplification of the details, but for the better part of a year and a half, I had to pay attorneys' fees to answer the suit that dragged on and on. All my attorney had to do, if the judge would let him, was to present the paperwork that exonerated me and I could be dismissed, but time and again the judge simply would not look this far into the case.

As much as you try and keep your mind out of a situation you can't do much about—or are paying your lawyer to handle for you—I couldn't stop thinking of the lawsuit. A lawsuit predicated by a series of events that had nothing to do with me and had all happened well before I even came into possession of my agency. A lawsuit that my attorney had irrefutable proof of my innocence. A lawsuit where time and again the judge halted my attorney from introducing his evidence. A lawsuit prompted by a simple inquiry of information I had a right to have.

I am not prone to rage, I am a rather even-keel kind of a guy, but as the situation wore on from a couple of months to six, to a year, my patience and my finances were wearing thin. I felt like I was the poster-boy for the financial crisis. It was as if the powers that be had found an unknowing scapegoat in little old Jeff Arnold. As if, come hell or high water—water that was increasingly swirling ever higher over my head—the trustee was going to find his guilty party in me.

I had to work my business. I had to grow the agency, keep the clients satisfied, and work to pay off the money I had borrowed against my house in good faith. Finally, near a year in, my attorney was able to introduce the evidence exonerating me. The judge had read all the complaints, motions, and points of law and finally got to my evidence . . . and still, it took another four months after he read my attorney's papers to dismiss me! Obviously, I had nothing to do with any of this, but man, what an ordeal it all was having to surf those legal waters for so long. In fact, the most ironic twist of all came as a direct result of me trying to cut the family's finances and pay those damn lawyer's fees. This is almost too good to be true, but I swear it happened.

In our attempt to downsize, my wife and I sold our big house for a smaller one. The agency was doing well and I was obviously back where I belonged, loving selling insurance all over again, but our expenses were such that it made no sense to keep such a big house. We looked for and found a smaller but beautiful home not far from our other one and made the deal to buy it.

Wouldn't you know, the house belonged to the very judge who had presided over my suit. If you don't think truth is stranger than fiction, you haven't lived long enough on this planet.

Extricated from under that kerfuffle, I got both my feet under me again and faced the new climate of selling insurance in the new century. The selling, of course, hadn't changed, but technology had grown by leaps and bounds, and people were certainly tighter with their money. But as has always been the case in the dream fulfillment business we are all in, people need insurance.

I amassed a solid group of good people around me, kept to the niche that I was comfortable with, and sullied forth. This second time around I also pushed hard to create a specific culture I wanted around me. I liken it to a kaizen process, one that I fitted into my way of looking at things. Yes, my employees and I would always be working toward "continual improvement," but not in the way I felt it was usually measured.

Business writer Michael Gerber suggests looking forward and visualizing things as you want them to be in your business, but he doesn't work with that mission statement view of life. What I gleaned from his books, tapes, and even seminars I attended, as well as what I learned early on through my faith, when it came to restarting in 2008, you tend to lose sight of what's important if you just follow charts, pipeline predictions, and continue to pass out inspiring pamphlets at endless board (which quickly become bored) meetings. What was important to me when building RIGHTSURE, my second insurance agency, was creating a culture in my shop. If I managed to do this correctly, then even when I was not in the office, even when I wasn't overseeing everything directly, my business would still run according to the parameters I'd set up. The culture I cultivated would thrive, and furthermore, my people could grow.

I have an ego just like the next guy; ask my wife, and she'll tell you I have probably too much of it to spare. But growing RIGHTSURE, I came to see that we are all best served by focusing more on the culture of treating our customers, our carriers, and one another well—and less on our individual egos.

How does this relate to buying and selling?

First of all, the healthier the culture we grew, the more successful RIGHTSURE became. Everyone felt part of something that they cared about and knew the company had their back. Morale was and still is good around my offices. I care for everyone I come in contact with, and the feeling is reciprocated.

Second, we came to respect those agencies we bought, as agency buying—as you have seen by now—quickly became a big part of what we did.

We also worked hard to maintain good relationships with our carriers. Yes, our customers are important, but so, too, are the carriers we sell who insure them. I need to know that if I come up against some hiccup, and as you know hiccups in the insurance business often have heavy dollar signs attached to them, I can get a carrier on the phone fast who will attend to my problem.

And last, we came to learn a most important fact: culture eats strategy. The best-laid plans will wither and die across a barren, uninspiring landscape.

This ethos also bleeds through in our deals, which is something I am proud of. I've been introduced, on more than one occasion, to business guru Simon Sinek's Golden Circle diagram. In his many talks, Sinek sketches a three-circle diagram, the outermost layer being the "what," the middle layer the "how," and the inner layer, the core, is the "why." It's not all as hippie vibe-y as it sounds. Take a company like Disney or Apple. Their "what" is what they are selling: Disney—toys, theme-park vacations, movies; Apple—personal electronic devices; at RIGHTSURE it is insurance.

That next step in, the "how," is a little trickier. But this can be seen in Disney tying in movie franchise acquisitions with theme parks, such as the toy/theme park tie-in they are executing now that they own *Star Wars*; Apple developing their iPhones and changing the music business with iTunes; and RIGHTSURE challenging the old style of our industry by using technology to the fore.

But that last bit, the "why," the innermost ring, is tougher to define but sits at the core of what Sinek calls those truly innovative successful companies. In fact, he postulates that a successful company always has a strong why, a reason for being, beyond hoping to sell ever more widgets.

For me, it is easy to define RIGHTSURE's why. It has always been my bottom-line desire to help people, pure and simple; this fuels what I do. Call it my background in the gospel, my general decency, or maybe even a wonderful need to delude myself, but for me, I have always seen what I do as helping people and, by extension, helping them to better protect themselves and their families. This idea, our why, informs the culture at RIGHTSURE and prompts how we do things. Yes, making money is important, but it does not supersede that why. In fact, you will read how I have had occasion to add lots of commas and zeros to my personal checkbook, but when the super-lucrative deal dangling before me went against what I knew would be best for RIGHTSURE, I didn't take it. I work hard not to let anything muck up the process of us doing what we can to best help people.

This is how and why my company gets deeply involved in the charity work we do. It's the simple idea of giving back, of as much recognizing the good fortune we have had as working beyond simply writing policies to help people. Through the years RIGHTSURE has been fortunate enough to build over ten houses, not just to write the checks for supplies and manpower, but to actually go down and assist with the building of houses in Mexico.

A gentleman by the name of Chris Petersen, who I can't thank enough, twisted my arm three or four times before I finally went with him on my first trip. I was overwhelmed by what I saw. The poverty the people there existed in was truly unimaginable; they had no running water, no electricity. I worked three long days that first time, built a foundation, a roof, and four walls so a family of five had a house . . . a two-room house measuring 10 X 10 with no water and no electricity, BUT IT WAS A HOUSE!

I returned from that trip and cried in my shower for fifteen minutes, I was so overwhelmed with what I had seen. It was startling to realize— but a good wake-up call to what's important in life—that the only difference between me and those impoverished folks in Mexico was that I had the good fortune to be born a few hours north in America, and could have everything and anything I could ever want by simply working smarter and harder. The people I met, thrilled to have that small, ill-equipped little home built for them, had nothing, and no amount of working harder or smarter on their part would ever matter due to the economic conditions and the lack of free market enterprise they lived in.

Forget the soapbox; I am not trying to make a political statement here. I was just smacked back into reality from what Chris showed me. Since that first trip, RIGHTSURE has built nine other houses in Mexico, and each time the process is more gratifying. This is certainly one of the most truly emotional journeys we take each year.

RIGHTSURE also sponsors classrooms in local schools every year and has contributed over one hundred thousand dollars to local schools. I feel these are the places that need our charity dollars most. I can't abide kids going without; it cuts me to the quick. Sometimes we make donations to schools and other times directly to teachers so they can stock their classrooms without the hassle of submitting a proposal to a school, as they often have to do. We simply cut out the middleman and fund their rooms personally. I don't have much time or respect for bureaucracies that tend to halt forward progress with their red tape and micromanaging. The resources we have can get supplies into the hands of those who need them most, and I take advantage where I can when I can to simply get things done.

Our local Gospel Rescue Mission for the homeless receives our corporate and personal donations as well as personal clothing and shelter items. Local homes for elderly women (widowed or just alone) also receive funds and volunteer hours from us annually. And we prepare thousands upon thousands of meals at our local community food bank in a group setting where the RIGHTSURE staff challenge one another to set records from prior years. All of this is rewarding work.

Literally a dozen entities are supported by either our volunteer hours, cash donations, or corporate resources. But the real blessing is when these things are done in secret, not for personal gloating or grandstanding (as I seem to be doing here, I know). Truly, we don't give for the recognition or accolades; we give because it's part of our core—my "why" of *helping people*— it's the right thing to do. With all that we are blessed with, not giving would be hoarding or stealing, as far as I see it.

You do what you will with your time and resources. I will do what I will with mine.

The point of all this is that I thought it best to remind you who you might come to deal with if ever our paths meet and you consider selling to me. Being aware of and cultivating our company's culture as positively as we have always tried to do, one easily recognizes how a newly acquired agency impacts RIGHTSURE. Hoping to only ever have our impact be a positive one, I discriminate on who we buy. Surely not every purchase has been a 100% win-win, especially in the beginning of our buying. But I am not knocking at your door, making an offer to buy your agency or even considering doing so if I do not think you won't be a good fit for RIGHTSURE.

For me, this has always been about more than feeding the coffers. I have to believe in what I do.

In a bit, you will come to the section on seller demands, and you will see clear evidence of how I come to respect and regard my seller beyond what is down on our contract. You will come to see quite clearly how the acquisition of a new agency is about more than just a numbers game, and you will see why I have to do the best job I can.

Chapter 5

Buying: The Deeper Dive

"What one thing, if solved, would transform our industry?"
Jeff Arnold

The total number of acquisitions we have been engaged in so far is sixty-two. Most of these were insurance agencies or brokerages, and a few were insurance companies. Many involved publicly traded companies, and three of my deals were with billion-dollar parent corporations. I wasn't successful at all of them, and some were as small as a $23,000 deal, while others required investments totaling $100 million.

I think it would be safe to say that a number as high as sixty-two speaks to the fact that I'm not a deal snob. I like all opportunities and learn as much from the small retail transactions as I do from the multistate multioffice conglomerates. I enjoy the chase, I won't kid you. It thrills me trying to massage a deal into place, enduring the back-and-forth negotiations, learning as much as I can about owners and agencies, applying my particular brand of technological research. Still, as I told you in the previous chapter, I discriminate in the size of agencies I buy and would rather deal within my insurance niche. And although I decidedly approach buying agencies in what I feel is a unique way, I don't throw the baby out with the bathwater when it comes to that history of selling I mentioned previously. I use those older concepts to keep me level-headed when delving into the complicated maneuverings of modern buying, reminding me as they do of different ways of getting things done, and also reminding me that, in many cases, many people still look at these old models as the way to sell their agency.

But to my way of thinking, a buyer misses much of the value of an agency by looking only at that assets/income/market model mentioned previously. In fact, often, after my assessment of an agency, the seller uses my offer to parlay a larger price from a completely different buyer. Yes, I realize that by being the first one at the table with a juicy offer, quite often we've lost a deal. This is the risk of doing things the way I do it. Still, I wouldn't do what I do any other way.

The number I come to is generally accepted as a well-considered bid by my competitors; they know I do a deep dive into all aspects of a seller's business, going well beyond the old way of looking at things. This is why I always tell sellers to keep whatever price they may think their agency is worth close to their chest. I repeat this caution time and time again because so many sellers, in their anxiousness, will too often tip their hand. I'm happy to report quite often a seller is pleasantly surprised at the number we quote them, as often it is a quote higher than the seller came to themselves.

No, I don't offer crazy amounts I know are foolish investments. Believe me, I am in this business to make money and to stick around for a long time. But I am willing to pay handsomely for healthy shops with hearty potential, whether paying an agency's owner out over time or in one lump sum. Taking into consideration that I might as much pay for an agency outright as I could over time, sellers realize that I am open to the many ways one might do a deal. Another little nugget of wisdom I find myself repeating is, **no two deals are alike**. If all parties acknowledge this fact, then neither will hold too tightly to what has gone before nor will they stand so steadfastly to expectations that they lose sight of the good of the deal before them.

I liken my process of buying a brokerage to a homeowner buying a house. The potential homeowner measures the house's lot, sees if the roof is sound, counts the number of bathrooms, and explores the basement to see if the foundation has any telltale signs of water leakage. But the home buyer should also take into account other factors outside of the structure of the house, factors that can only be determined with a look beyond the property and a deeper consideration of his specific needs. If the homeowner has young kids, shouldn't she be exploring the school system in the area? How about those rumors she's been hearing of a new bus stop going in only a block from the property? The main street downtown area seems to be undergoing a revitalization; will that add to the crowds in a good or bad way? How about the rumor of a huge condo village being built off the two-lane road just down the street; will the traffic suddenly be murder around town?

See my point? Simply looking at the house—your book—does not tell me the whole story of how sound this deal might be for me. Surely, I am extremely interested in your commissions, the actual numbers you are bringing in. I want to know what carriers you have and how many clients you have signed up, and who is set for renewal—your roof, number of bathrooms, whether your water heater needs to be replaced. But I also consider the potential of your carriers and clients, where your shop might be located and the economic health of the area around you, the types of insurance you sell and your reputation. I am not saying you haven't considered these things, but I am coming from a different place than you, executing my research specific to my needs.

And in many cases the value I find in my deep dive is about how I can come to make lemonade out of seeming lemons, all because of the strength of RIGHTSURE's place in the business.

Remember, when selling your agency, while it is imperative to come to a price, the value of an agency matters only with how much someone is willing to pay for it. Even projected sky-high profits wouldn't tickle me to consider an agency; yes, they can figure in, but I look at numbers from many different angles. I have been involved in big money deals where I have had to partner with other agencies, search for funding to close a deal, etc. But in those deals, I too often found lots of queen bees but no worker bees. The amount of time it all took, crunching zeros as well as mollifying egos, and how much I was anchored to my cell phone at all hours and even during the weekend when I'd rather be playing with my kids, was not worth my effort. Maybe I am, as I have always thought of myself, just a regular, humble dude, but I have come to find making deals over a certain amount isn't in my DNA.

Of course, into this full mix is a host of other factors a buyer considers, beyond your EBITDA or the other factors mentioned above. Here's where I fasten the scuba gear on and get into my deep diving.

Type of Carriers You Have

At the top of this "tree" is my question of whether you are a captive agency—meaning you sell for only one carrier—or independent. This will determine if I can even buy your shop, as RIGHTSURE is an independent agency and as such can and only wants to buy other independents. If you are indeed an independent and looking to sell, then we can climb down the tree a smidgen and consider the carriers you represent, specifically if they are national, regional, and niche insurance providers.

The big players in our industry, the national carriers, certainly add to your brokerage's cache if you happen to sell for them. I am bound to be quite interested in how many of these types of carriers you have, as name brand recognition in our field is as important as it is in many other industries. These agencies offer healthy commissions—because they are big enough to do so—and in lots of instances would-be insureds come to or will want to stay with these companies because of the carrier's reputation or because of well-known advertising campaigns or simple family history with these brands. Also, I know that these carriers tend to be discriminating in who sells for them because they can be, and whatever made your brokerage attractive to these carriers makes you attractive to me. I might have specific personal feelings about some of the big boys, good or bad, but I can't deny who they are and how discriminating they can be. There is a behind-the-scenes valuation here that necessitates my deep diving.

This does not mean, though, that I will not be interested in your agency have you only regional agencies or a larger percentage of them over national.

In my experience, some of the best regional carriers manage to pay agencies lucrative yearly commissions and are often wonderful carriers. These regional carriers not only present a strong presence in the specific area they are located, but they are hungry, in the sense that they are in many cases on the cusp of breaking out to be a national carrier and working damn hard to exploit that potential. This hunger makes them invariably flexible and nimble in their everyday dealings . . . and who wouldn't want to get into bed with a carrier like this?

These regional carriers don't rely on some Wall Street marketing firm they retain to take the temperature of the industry for them; they are out there themselves working their given region of the country. If I come to buy your agency and have some trouble with one of your ex-clients trying to work through a clerical hiccup or even have to argue a fraud claim, I know my chances are good that I could get the CEO of a regional carrier on the phone or even down to my office (I often have) before the you-know-what hits the fan. Sure, I'll probably lose this kind of access when this regional insurance company goes national, that's the nature of the business; I'd never damn someone for wanting to grow or aspire to be bigger and better. But for right now you can see why your good relationship with a regional carrier is attractive to me.

Last on this tree, I consider the niche branch. As with my consideration between captive and independent agencies making or breaking a deal for me, depending on how niche your niche, I might not be able to buy your agency.

Presently RIGHTSURE sells insurance for personal and small commercial risks and, even though technically speaking covering large truck hauling or aviation could be considered "vehicle insurance," I wouldn't know the first thing about how to approach policies in these fields. Therefore the niche you are in, even if it falls close to mine, might make it impossible for me to consider buying you. You know how the consumer sees these things: they look at a strip mall with, say, six or seven stores and figure one company or type of insurance covers these stores, and they would be right; we call it "mercantile" in our business. But to your potential buyer's way of thinking, even if I were a mercantile insurer, I would need to know what kind of businesses make up those storefronts. While I might be a big player in selling mercantile insurance, I might not know about the specifics of selling insurance to a walk-in emergency clinic or a movie theatre, and they might be among the niche among the niche here.

In the end what I want from the seller is the list of your carriers. In my due diligence, I will consider the insurance companies you sell and determine their value from the factors listed above. I also dive deep into correspondence between you and your carriers. While I'd rather have you and your insurance companies happy with one another, this is not always the case. But in a making-lemonade- from-lemons result of RIGHTSURE's particular thirty years in the insurance business, I am in good standing with so many carriers, both independent and national, that I can mend fences if need be. What might presently be a negative relationship between you and a carrier could easily turn into a healthy one with me as owner. Sure, it will take some time to massage this opportunity to full fruition, as you will read later in the "Behind the Scenes" section about how much time it can take to contact carriers. But from my particular deep dive into your present carrier relationships, I can often find positives, where to you there might only have seemed to be negatives for a long time.

Commissions

Knowing that no one carrier can be all things to all people—although many of them try to sell the public on this concept in the modern marketplace—I look at the commissions you make across the number of the carriers you sell. Also, knowing that bigger carriers can sometimes afford to give you a better percentage on your commissions, I look at all these numbers in relationship to what, in the end, serves your clients best. Your commissions will not impress me much if your clients are about to jump ship from carriers promising them the moon, not a fact you might tell me or even know, but one I can sometimes surmise from facts, figures, and what I know about our industry.

If clients don't renew, no further commissions are to be had. This revenue stream, which we count on most of all, just stops. At RIGHTSURE—and I'd have to imagine at every other smart insurance broker—we do everything in our power to keep the client feeling safe and secure, valued. But sometimes I don't even get the chance to work my magic on those new people I acquire from the sale.

In some cases I will simply lose your clients because you have sold to me and they don't know nor want to know me from Adam. In other cases, they might stay right where they are and never explore other insurance simply because they are skittish about the change of ownership or their assumptions that we can't handle whatever else they throw at us. It becomes a delicate seesaw to ride, so rest assured I am accessing your commission situation best I can when it comes to considering buying you or not.

Liquidity

Simply put, liquidity is the solvency vs. profitability end of what is presented in your financials. More than how much money I can make from a potential commission, here I am considering how much cash you want up front against how much debt your agency might owe. Not everybody comes to me with debt, but I have been burned by not looking into the possibility that an agency might have debt. Yes, I know this agency is your baby, you've nursed it, cared for it, and want it to grow, but a baby with two broken arms and a broken leg might not be the kind of baby I want to get to know or will need to swaddle ever so creatively.

I as much look at who you might owe (I will get into UCC filings in a bit, and how important they are so a buyer can figure out who a seller might owe beyond who the seller *says* they owe) as how I might best pay off those debts when I acquire your shop. In some cases, as you will read in the next paragraph, I can even benefit from acquiring a broker's debt and paying it promptly.

I once bought an agency that was valued at $750,000 but owed $600,000 in debt to the Yellow Pages; phone calling is essential to our business. Still wanting this agency even with their debt-heavy balance sheet, I ended up giving the seller $92,000 up front and taking on their debt. But acting proactively, I called one of the six Yellow Pages the agency owed, got them to stop the interest accruing by setting up a monthly plan to pay them, and in effect I gained a free loan.

Again, only a deep dive will have one come to see the advantages of a situation that seems to have no silver lining.

High vs. Low Risk

Just as there are high-risk policies and higher risk insureds, there are higher risk agencies. If you happen to be one, you might not so readily admit or even realize it.

For instance, if you insure men and women in their midtwenties and these clients pay cash on a month-by-month basis, you are high risk. Your offer might be $.75–$.92 on the dollar, where if you were a low-risk agency with a client base in its fifties mostly on direct deposit from their bank accounts, your offer could be in the realm of $2.25–$3.00 on the dollar.

Again, the heavily advertised big brand-name insurance carriers queered the field here. In attempting to provide all kinds of coverage to all kinds of people for all kinds of needs, the all-over-the-map-grab-everybody-no-matter-what business model means lots of high-risk people presently insured and brokerages trying to insure them to keep up with the big boys.

I need to surf all this and consider who and what you have and not let prejudice slip in over mere terms like high risk or low risk. Each situation is different and needs a deep dive on my part.

I Want to KISS You

Please understand, I have worked hard at simplifying my approach. I take the KISS axiom when it comes to explaining my deep diving: Keep It Simple, Stupid. I am the stupid one in the equation here, though; not you: Stupid if I can't find a way to explain my methods succinctly; stupid if what I do takes up too much of your time; stupid if I can't convince you that my approach will be better for you in the end. Yes, I came from the IT end of town. My agency works at a high-efficiency level using all the latest technology, working through big deals of millions of dollars. But I pride myself on being able to sit across from a seller who has never been in this position before and wants nothing more than to have the process over and done with so they can play with their grandkids. Making it clear how I came to my offer and how it is the best offer that will ever cross the table for this seller's agency is something I need to do succinctly, honestly, and simply, I know.

Now that you have come to the valuation, the price you feel is fair for what your agency, don't be surprised if you come to some disagreement—with a few people even—over how much your agency is worth. I believe in potential, but it needs to be realistic, and my deep dive keeps me always considering the actual numbers that I could make with your agency in the future. Surely, no one can ever predict these future earnings with pinpoint accuracy, but I'll be able to tell if, in the end, there is enough there for me to do a deal with you.

Countless times I have been the first one to offer a valuation only to have it parlayed against a second or third offer from other buyers, the seller pushing for an even higher price. This proactive "go-getter-ism" has served my company well, but I would need lots more fingers and toes to count how many times I wish I would not have responded so quickly. You'd think I'd learn by now not to be so anxious; it's what I always caution sellers against after all!

Let me digress for a moment with two cautionary tales. Our homework needs to be complete on every level. The art of the deal is bound in **what you know** of that deal, from as many pathways as you can know it, and not what you *feel* about it. Admittedly, I am a product of the Kentucky Public School system, and perhaps I learn things slower, but in the two nightmare deals I am about to relate to you, I came to learn the hard way. One of these hard lessons learned happened before my agency was bought by that big bank and one after when I got back into the business again. Thrown for a loop in each instance, surely it was hard to admit my folly when I saw what I had wrought. But I have come to humbly regard these two mistakes as not only something a buyer can learn from—and I was the buyer in both instances—but something a seller can take caution from as well.

As I mentioned, I was known in those early years of owning my agency as the IT-guy-to-go-to when it came to the early intersection of technology and insurance. This was the midnineties, way before you could watch a tutorial on YouTube, hire somebody, or manage your own Google searches for whatever ailed you. My firm was a pioneer in implementing technology with the intricacies of insurance. In fact, we were written up in *Forbes* and *The Wall Street Journal* for how we were able to get "DocuSign" into our work, how we faxed applications and bound our laptops to this cutting-edge side of the business. I guess my mom buying me a Texas Instruments and Commodore 64 computer when I was fourteen and me taking it apart and putting it back together again, adding memory chips, paid off.

Quite often I'd find myself down at my local Bruegger's Bagels, sipping my morning coffee and holding court for an ever-rotating grouping of insurance agents coming in to pick my brain. I didn't charge for this; it wasn't consulting on any kind of well-thought-out level. I just liked sharing what I knew. And given my performance background, I liked being "on" in this way.

During these informal meet-ups, I came in contact with two guys, partners in an insurance agency, who I came to know well. After not so much time I learned they were looking to sell their agency. These guys weren't what you would call the best of friends. In fact, I think the longer they stayed in business, the more what little affection they had had for one another whittled away (hey, it happens). Given this, it was no surprise that the last thing they wanted was for one of them to sell the agency to the other; nobody was going to get the upper hand in any way here. When I learned that they wanted out and that they were adamant about NOT selling to each other, I figured, hey, I could buy them, right? But I didn't do my due diligence. I didn't even conduct a basic UCC filing search.

I had the cash on hand to buy, and I simply assumed the statements I was given by those two men reflected their agency's financials completely. But this firm happened to be "out of trust," a term we all know, and I only ever got a look at their payroll, not their current statements of what they owed to their insurance carriers . . . and they owed a lot. Within a week of buying this agency, my office received demand letters from most of those insurance carriers the firm owed, a debt *I* now owed since I had bought the agency. I might have had the money to buy the firm, but God knows I didn't have the money to pay off this debt right then and there.

Luckily, I had a solid reputation at that point, as I had been in business five years, with an unblemished record. One of the insurance companies the old agency owed was one I worked with—and had a great relationship with—and for them and the other creditors demanding their balances I was able to offer a 180-day payout schedule. I indeed paid off all the debt within this time, but I had to cut staff to do so, and that financial and personal hit was not something I ever wanted to go through again.

Live and learn, right?

Well . . .

Jump ahead ten years. I was on my second go-around owning an agency, the very agency I own now. I had bought countless agencies along the way by this point, big and small. I was actively buying to such a degree that I had a well-worn system in place for my deals, a template I first developed on paper and over the years written down into a concise computer program for vetting potential sales. Let's just say I'd been to the rodeo aplenty.

As we all know, in any business, even with the most cursory of networking, you come across either friends or competitors, coworkers, many people who do what you do. I had occasion to cross paths with a mature lady who was a big name in our industry and heard rumblings that she was looking to sell her agency. She had a few personal matters that were demanding, stuff that when she told you about it your heart bled for this woman and her family. She had to get out fast so she could attend to her family, and I was completely sympathetic. Or should I say, blinded?

I decided that, in this woman's case, I would skip through my usual multipage checklist, put together the cash, and make her an offer. Yes, here I was, Mr. Experience being swayed by the emotional impact of this woman's story, thinking that I could manage a quick good deal for everyone concerned. I was just trying to help. I had a sense of all this by now, right? I could sniff out a solid deal, couldn't I?

Stupid, I know.

Papers signed, deal done, I come to learn, from none other than the IRS, that this woman could not sell. She had avoided paying taxes for seven years—something the government doesn't take to all that well—and had a lien against her business. I couldn't buy it, although I already had! Luckily, I had worked into our deal a right of offset. Still, at the end of the day, I was out tens of thousands of dollars.

Develop a protocol, a checklist, a template for either buying or selling born from your due diligence, and stick to it. Freestyling when it comes to matters like these, where there is so much money on the table and the future of your business and what you might be able to set up for your family, is not a good idea. The big takeaway lessons here are: **keep to your protocol,** how you normally figure your deal; **take every seller on a case-by-case basis, knowing that what you think you may know is never all there is to know;** and last, **don't buy (or sell even) with your emotions;** numbers should be the only thing ever driving a deal.

Hard lessons all, and in these two cases above, costly. But at the root of the mistakes here was how I failed to do my due diligence.

Seller Demands

I have found that no matter the type of sale we put together—stock sale, completing buying an agency's book with all the money paid in one lump sum upfront, an incentivized buyout—there can come what I call seller demands. These are simple, nonenforceable requests, some strongly made, beyond what is written down on a contract. This does not make these seller wishes any less legitimate or important for me to try and make possible, though.

I have seen everything from a seller wanting us to be open certain hours, to making sure we always have certain candy available in little bowls around the conference room, to, in one case, a seller requesting that a bowl of water was always set out—bottled water, that is—if and when customers came into the office with their dog. I take all these demands seriously because I know that the seller is not asking for these things to simply try and queer our deal or drive me to distraction.

He or she kept their agency's doors open certain hours, or maybe one of their clients-soon-to-be-one-of-my-clients has a dog that they like to bring into the insurance office from time to time. Sure, there are times sellers are looking to keep their hands in; it's human nature for any of us to fantasize exerting a little control on something we used to control but do not control any longer. But I can tell you from experience that in most of these instances, demands are made simply because a seller wants to maintain their legacy, even to a small degree.

Of course for the seller who has fashioned a buyout deal with us (see below), it behooves me to treat their clients the way they want because we are both still in the deal together for me to make as much money for them as possible. Simply put, satisfying their client base is best for all. But for even those sellers from whom I simply buy their book outright, it still matters to me that I do all I can to keep their legacy alive. I certainly won't do anything that runs counter to how RIGHTSURE does business, but I'm not the kind of buyer who hands over money per the deal, takes your agency, and then runs roughshod over what you built.

Sure, the buyer can promise the seller the moon and renege on every demand. Only what has been signed over in the contract is truly germane here, and these points about cold water in doggy dishes or specific hours of operation are usually not in the fine print. But I know what it means to build something you care about, and your agency was your life's work. I know fully well how you can come to care about people you consider as much friends as clients.

Types of Deals

There are so many ways to "do" the deal. I have been privy to a bunch, navigated some I wasn't even familiar with, and have heard about a lot more I never have, nor will I ever, try. For our purposes, I will explain the types of buying I get into most often and am therefore most familiar with. Again, I can't stress enough about having experts on hand to advise you on what will be best for your particular needs. Numbers drive a deal, this is true, but those numbers can fit into so many different types of buying and selling.

As mentioned before, determining the type of deal you want—how exactly you want to sell your agency, what you need for its sale, and what you need now or later for your finances—is as important as determining your agency's valuation and culling through a list of buyers. But as with everything else, nothing is written in stone. Quite often a little pushback from a buyer might see you changing the parameters of what you were initially hoping for, or that pushback might be enough for you to seek another buyer/deal entirely. Being flexible is good, but breaking entirely leaves the seller in a weak position. Also, I have seen a seller's demands and terms sometimes change when they have their agency up for sale and no one is buying; sometimes when nobody comes biting at your bait, you need to rehook it.

Usually, though, the seller wants to stick close to certain terms as well as price, just as there are certain aspects of each type of deal I will want if I were to have my druthers.

No matter the kind of deal we come to, trust is what matters most in the end. If you don't trust that I can deliver what I say I will for your agency, it doesn't matter what our terms are. But let's assume you have realized that I am trustworthy, smart, and will shepherd your agency well into the future—I'm not being conceited here; you will most likely come to this conclusion, as I have been doing this a long time and my reputation speaks to my integrity—then here is the most common type of deal that could be on the table:

The Asset Purchase. I told you before that those printers, desk chairs, all that stuff you have in your office will not amount to all that much. When I say assets here, I mean your book of business, the potential for your policy renewals. This is the true currency of any insurance brokerage as far as I am concerned—the clients who you have and how well they will renew in the future. Buying the book of business is the number one best way for me to buy an agency, and if I had my druthers, I would always proceed in this way. It's just that not all sellers are set up for this for various reasons we will see in a bit.

Also, there are times, on the high-end of the scale, where agencies are simply looking for a price I can't or more likely do not want to meet with cash on hand. At this point in the game, I have healthy relationships with banks and investment funds. I pay back my debts usually before they come due, and my reputation is such that I am not at all a risk to lenders; I can usually get whatever money is being asked, even if I wanted to go above my usual $7 million ceiling to buy an agency. But the more money I borrow, the more hoops I have to jump through. Pledging so much collateral against a loan; filling out what usually comes to nearly one-hundred-page contracts; tying me up with UCC filings; the loan weighing heavily on my balance sheet for the time it takes me to pay it off; and the sheer amount of time it takes for this process brings me more headaches than sometimes the deal is worth, I feel. Without borrowing, I can usually close a deal within three months.

I won't kid you, even when I don't have to borrow heavily, even when the sale is in the perfect price range for me, I have still gotten burned on this kind of sale. Through an error or omission in a seller's book of business, he or she might "forget" to add open-ended items, liabilities that I will come to take on as the buyer. This is why I come to this kind of sale with "tail coverage." The idea here is that everything has a tail attached to it and that if something untoward surfaces after I buy your agency, some unforeseen buried liability or one of those forgotten errors, my tail coverage insurance will see to it that I am covered, up to a certain amount of money.

It's that old theory of transferring risk to a third party, the very concept insurance is built on. In the case of tail coverage, I buy a policy from an insurance company who will step in to pay what ills surface. If I indeed set up a "first dollar defense" with this coverage, attorneys' fees are paid so that lawyers will step in to defend me right away if I get sued or served. Sometimes the seller and I split the cost for this insurance, but part of my due diligence is not to proceed without it.

The Stock Sale. This type of sale can be a risky proposition for the buyer. I have bought through a stock sale, but there is so much possibility for surprises here—never good surprises—that the stock sale is not something I take to all that often. Buying an agency's book is one thing, and as I described, omissions in that kind of a sale can come up to bite me. But with a stock sale, the buyer is grabbing the agency's entire stock holdings (shares), which means the buyer could also be acquiring all the seller's ills. Say for instance that the seller didn't file a payroll tax payment or didn't pay their health insurance for a year—everything and anything related to their business—I am now responsible for it as the buyer. Yes, there is tail insurance for this kind of a sale, but things get ever more complicated when it comes to a stock sale. I really don't like them.

The Buyout. To be clear here, technically there are two types of buyouts, but the result for the seller is the same; he or she is going to get the bulk of his money over time. There are many advantages for both the buyer and seller in a buyout, one of the biggest being how all parties can avoid larger tax repercussions. RIGHTSURE has always been on the up and up as far as Uncle Sam is concerned. As you read, I already "enjoyed" more than a year entangled in a suit I had no involvement in, and I never again need that kind of a headache, believe me! I pay my taxes, we keep meticulous accounting for anyone who cares to see it, and I have built years of trust in this business because of my proactive and honest approach. But if a seller and I can lessen a tax burden on us for our sale, something I know your CPA and attorney will be on board with, then why not work to this aim?

I promise I will get into some of the withering tax implications of buying and selling in a bit. For now, let's just say that lessening taxes is only one part of why a buyout works for many a seller and buyer.

Let me illustrate the merits of the buyout from a scenario I have often found myself in:

I want to buy your agency. You want me to buy your agency. But we can't meet at the price you want. We might be off only a half a million, not a lot of money considering the overall numbers we are talking here, but still the machinery of our deal is getting glunked-up over this amount. What often happens in these instances is that buyer and seller structure the terms of the deal for a buyout so that the amount they are not meeting on can be reached over time.

Now, who you are, or more precisely how you see your future, determines which of the two kinds of buyouts (those two being the incentivized/renewal buyout or the direct buyout) you will seek. In many cases, the seller/agency owner has invested well, has a sizeable income stashed, and is looking for the money I send them monthly as icing on a rich, wonderful cake. Maybe they have set up my payments to an education fund for the grandkids or to dip into for lavish vacations.

You can see why these folks want to slip out quietly, take the balance of their price over time so they can enjoy lower taxes than if they had taken one big lump sum, enjoy a steady stream of income coming at them from a reputable source over a finite period. For these people, a *direct buyout* works fine. They leave me to run their agency, trusting that I will pay them the remaining balance we agreed on beyond that small percentage of the price I paid at closing. We determine what I will pay out over a specific period, setting those payments up electronically with penalties installed on our end if we fail to remit on schedule (which I can report RIGHTSURE has never failed to do), and the deal is done.

Then there are other sellers, maybe close to the same age as the folks above, who are simply sick of the day-to-day headaches of running their office. Worrying about meeting payroll, surfing constant employee dramas, dealing with what new carrier is courting him or her, or how they have to go out and court a carrier, it all becomes too mind-numbing after a time, especially for those men and women nearing or over retirement age. But these people still love selling insurance. They love attending to clients they have had for years, are considered family in these people's homes. It does enliven you to feel that you impact people's lives on a regular basis, believe me I know. For these sellers, an *incentivized buyout* works better.

The incentivized or renewal buyout sees us agree, once again, on me paying you the remaining balance left from what I gave you at the time of sale, over time. But in this case, the percentage of that balance I pay you monthly is contingent upon your agency's performance under my new ownership. To be sure, you will certainly get the full amount you are owed; this is set in stone in the deal like in a regular buyout. But the amount of each individual payment is based on renewals and how well your ex-client base does under my care. "Incentivized" in this way, the seller can stand to make even quite a bit more money monthly than me paying him or her a fixed percentage price of the regular buyout. This is why an incentivized buyout is attractive to the seller who is still in the game, who still wants to sell insurance and simply wants me to take over the day-to-day running of the company.

As I mentioned, at the heart of all these deals, certainly in either buyout where you are waiting for me to pay you monthly, you need to trust me. Trust me to keep your customers not only happy but wanting to keep doing business with me. Trust me to grow your agency. And in the end, trust that I will do all of this even better than you did so I stay in business.

Chapter 6

Post Buy: My Behind-the-Scenes

"When companies experience authentic collaboration and intentional synergy, they become great."
Jeff Arnold

Some sellers do indeed grab a one-lump payment and get out of dodge. Other agency owners who take their one lump and splitsville still structure their terms in such a way that they want assurances that we will be taking care of their baby in the manner they see fit. These are the agency owners who want to know with absolute certainty that we'll always have that cold bottled water for dogs who come to visit us, that we will treat their customers the way they treated them, that RIGHTSURE's culture reflects their own.

Then still other folks sell to us but keep their hand in. They continue to work their clients, drawing a minimum salary even after we pay them a specific lump sum to buy their shop. Other folks have a vested interest in how we continue our business, as we will keep paying them out over time.

Whoever you are and however you deal (or don't deal) with RIGHT-SURE post the sale, I think what follows might be of interest. It's also interesting to note that much of what occurs behind the scenes for RIGHTSURE post your sale is a direct result, good and bad, of what I advised in the selling chapter on how to make your agency more lucrative before the sale.

My four main concerns for RIGHTSURE immediately after we sign the papers and take ownership of your agency are COMPLIANCE, AUDIT, RECONCILIATION, and NOTIFICATION. You will find all these concerns layer into one another in what we have to go through. If you think we managed a deep dive before, brother you ain't seen nothing yet!

Compliancy

In working my due diligence for compliance, I need all of your files. This is where that "make it all digital" rule pays off dividends and why, way back when as I came to consider your agency, if you did not have all your files digitized I might have balked at buying it. I need passwords, the signed applications of all your clients, more or less everything. Sooner more than later I will be reaching out to tickle renewals. I'll be NOTIFYING clients, maybe prompting those who are overdue with a payment. I'll come to try and sell them on something else or, at the very least, a client will call RIGHTSURE and I will need to impress upon them that in the changeover of ownership, all is still working as efficiently as it ever did.

RIGHTSURE gives great exit calls to each customer—the old, the new, the disgruntled, or the deliriously happy. But we can't maintain this high standard without my agents knowing all they can about our clients. You know as well as I, no customer wants to be kept on hold or feel like they are not given anything less than the most personal attention possible, especially when they come to learn their brokerage has changed owners.

These first few months of the changeover, certainly for clients who might come to renew, add to what can be a mighty delicate time. I need all the information you have to do my job best I can.

And for those clients who have life insurance policies, there is a whole host of state and federal rules I need to follow in contacting them. I can't do this unless I know who those clients are and what exactly their policies entail.

I also need to contact your carriers, NOTIFYING them who I am and that I now own your agency.

"Yeah, so what, Jeff," I hear you say, "That's kinda the deal, isn't it? You just bought my agency; you will have to contact the carriers I used to represent. This is buying 101, no?" Well, if you think all this contacting is done via a phone call or email, think again. First of all, in many cases, the carrier has no idea who I am. Few will be notified before our deal is done (remember I told you to keep strict confidentiality about your selling to anyone but potential buyers), and plenty more simply don't read emails or return phone calls. I can't begin to tell you how many carriers demand I get in touch via fax or certified mail who ignore my faxes or mail. In the best case scenario, I might finally get in contact with the carrier by the third try; worst case . . . well, I don't even want to tell you how many times I had to try to contact one carrier until I finally got to talk to them.

Audit

The buck stops here about the bucks stopping here now that I own your agency. Certainly, I have done a deep dive into your finances—best I could—as we negotiated the sale of your agency. But now that your finances are mine, you can be assured I will go over your commissions and bank statements and match my spreadsheets. This is the only real way I can predict the future of these earnings I just acquired to make informed projections.

I need to know who is renewing on your list of clients, who I might work on to move over to a different carrier that will give me a better deal for that client going forward; checking the yield spread overall, I begin my micro-targeting. Overall, I need to make sure I spend my money to create a better experience for those customers I just acquired. I truly need to keep them renewing with me to make RIGHTSURE the most money we can down the line.

I also need to update accounting. I can't begin to tell you how many carriers keep paying the old agency owner, having no clear idea he/she has sold. Many times the carrier's accounting department doesn't catch the changeover. Presently I have thousands owed me from an old owner who has been getting paid from carriers, but RIGHTSURE has owned his agency for the past six months!

Reconciliation and Notification

All of the above speaks of reconciliation: reconciling the accounts you gave us, commission due us, data downloaded. It's one thing to order a box of one hundred widgets and when only fifty get delivered the error can all too easily be determined and rectified. But with what we are buying here, there is a limited time of offset, and time is of the essence to make sure we ring that bell correctly the first time with your ex-customers, who are now ours. And we need to get going, making sure all the numbers match up so we can make bigger numbers in our future.

By sheer errors and omission, too many things can slip by. Let me give you a real example.

During the last week of you owning your agency, through all the chaos and you dreaming about that RV and heading to sights unseen, one of your customers happens through your doors. As he has always done, this twenty-something guy pays his renewal with a check a day or two before his policy cancels. As I postulate here, your office is in disarray from the sale, there are as many celebrations as clandestine meetings between associates, and although that customer's renewal check is received and deposited in your account, someone in your office fails to notify the carrier. For all practical purposes, although this customer has paid, this customer is not insured. Yes, he did pay his premium, he came in before the allotted time was due, and he believes he is covered. But he isn't because the money was never reported to the carrier from your office.

Guess what happens to this customer when he leaves your office. Bam, he gets in a car accident.

He files a claim. He's got a solid policy of collision and theft for his Honda. Nobody got hurt in the accident and it wasn't even his fault, so he figures he will put the claim through and his insurance company, reputable and straight-as-an-arrow with this customer for as long as he has had them, will pay. Heck, his agent (you) has been wonderful to him for as long as he's known you. What could be easier?

A week goes by, and our twenty-something dude gets a letter telling him that his policy has been canceled due to nonpayment. But the guy remembers walking down to your office as he always did, flirting with your secretary as he always did, and handing off his check.

RIGHTSURE now owns your agency. This customer is ours. He'll be calling us soon enough to inquire about this letter he got from his insurance carrier. Can I stand on ceremony and blame you, the ex-owner, that in the confusion of selling you didn't contact the carrier that this client had paid? In my first week owning your accounts, it's not going to be prudent (and the heck with that, it's just not right!) for me to pass the buck. How quickly will I lose our twenty-something Honda owner if I spin this all off on "the old owner"? I need to go to bat for this client, who is now my client. It's up to me to fight for him, to represent him in good stead, and explain to the carrier what happened.

I went through something much like this in our office recently. In fact, I had to bring five other agents in on a call that lasted for two hours, all to get a client's concerns answered. That's a lot of RIGHTSURE agent power that could have been off doing other RIGHTSURE business during that time. But the error in the client's account had occurred through an error of omission, and it was on me to work out the problem. We have to always be working to assist the customer, that's our bottom line.

Now you understand why reconciliation of even the most minute points is extremely important.

Most of the stickiness or failure in the systems above is nobody's fault, per say. It's normal human error, or maybe a little complacency, lack of manpower, or maybe somebody simply forgets to call me back. I get it. I run a big operation. I know there are plenty of factors you can't be on top of, in all the same way, 24/7. But what I am aware of, and what will stop me cold in my tracks, is knowing that a) We might be losing money from some clerical error, b) We don't have all the information from the seller we need, or c) A client will contact RIGHTSURE for the first time, and if we don't have the proper information to treat their call in an exemplary manner and impress upon them that they are our top priority, we can't unring that bell, and they might be off looking for the land of little green geckos or hummable end-of-commercial taglines.

Chapter 7

Tax Implications: Uncle Sam Takes His Cut

"Well done is better than well said."
Benjamin Franklin

Although I touched on this quagmire in the "Deals" section above, I'd like to discuss more about taxes here. This is important stuff, and I would be remiss to not explore this in the best way I can.

Frankly, I'm not sure there is any part of a deal where both seller and buyer should be more simpatico. Sure, you want to come to an agreement on the price; you'll have no deal if you don't. But it's been my experience that no matter the type of deal that goes down, both parties and the amount of money gained or given, both parties want to keep Uncle Sam from slipping his hand too far into their pockets. In every instance, seller and buyer both will help themselves greatly by marshaling their forces, looking deeply at their needs, and agreeing to some basics so they can keep the tax man at bay, legally of course.

If taxes are not handled creatively and with a strict eye on detail, both buyer and seller (especially the seller) might leave the deal with quite a bit less than they might have initially been hoping for. In fact, I have heard it quoted that sellers who do not explore long-term tax implications with a good tax attorney or accountant can lose as much as 50% of what they could have made in their sale. As a buyer, I also do not want to be left with less than I could have gotten if I had just managed some basics, or at the very least, listened to my CPA.

Don't take my word for it. Read what I lay out below, then talk to those experts you hired; here's where they will earn the money you pay them. Listen wisely as your accountant and lawyer walk you through what you can do and what you can't when it comes to taxes and selling. Hit them with the questions you have from what you read here, from the rumors you have heard, from what you have come to learn and are hoping from your research; explore every avenue. I can only give you these lessons from my experience, and even vast as it might be, every state has different laws, and each buyer and seller's situation is unique.

There are so many ways to legally get the best from the taxes that will be leveled on you. Certainly I don't explore every aspect of tax implications below, but following is an overview of what to consider and explore further with your team. And when it comes to tax considerations, seller and buyer should be presenting a united front to try and bolster both their positions against the IRS. It's not as much an adversarial relationship I am proposing (when it comes to such large figures it's just plain dumb to be making an enemy of the IRS) as one where seller and buyer and their respective advisors look out for one another.

C Corporations vs. S Corporations

Your business probably falls into one of these two categories (or an LLC). For our purposes here, let's explore the good and the bad of each, the C Corp. and the S Corp., when it comes to the taxes you pay. The C and S distinction stands for nothing more than how U.S. corporations are delineated in the IRS Code.

A C Corporation is subject to double taxation. One is a tax at the corporate level (the IRS taxes the corporation's net income); the second tax is levied against the corporation's shareholders when they share in the company's profits. Yes, I know this sounds like IRS double dipping, but consider that the C Corp. can take a maximum of tax deductions and expenses within this double-taxed structure. Employee benefits especially can be enjoyed to the full extent of tax exemptions, as the C corp. can deduct from programs like medical reimbursements and many other employee benefits.

But remember, with a C Corp., even if the money you get for selling your agency is taken out over time—the incentivized buyout, for instance—it is still doubly taxed.

An S Corporation is only ever under one level of taxation from good old Uncle Sam. All income of this kind of corporation is spread out among the shareholders of the company, and they get taxed by the flow-through of those taxes personally. A one-time tax like this sounds like a good idea, yes, but there are many restrictions on S Corporations: owner/employees holding 2% or more of the company's shares cannot receive tax-free benefits, the company can only offer one class of stock, to name a few. There are no such restrictions on a C Corp.

Maybe the IRS figures they can keep their hands off a C Corp. when they are paying double taxes?

Here is a breakdown of the numbers for both a C Corp. and an S Corp. on a million-dollar deal.

If the seller is a C corporation, the agency could pay a tax rate as high as $340,000 on a capital gain of $1 million. The state will want its cut as well, so assuming the corporate state tax rate is 5% in the seller's state, the seller could pay an additional $50,000 in taxes on that mil. The corporation now has $610,000 to distribute to shareholders (who will be taxed now because in a C corporation, both the company and the shareholders get taxed), and they will pay capital gains tax on that $610,000, which could be as high as 20% or $122,000. The shareholders will also have to pay a state sales tax, again let's assume it is 5% ($30,500), and the Obama Care Tax, which could be as high as 3.8% or a cool $23,180. The shareholder on this million-dollar deal then walks away with $434,320, less than half of the sale price.

Is your head spinning yet?

The same deal million-dollar sale for an S Corp.?

The one million capital gain flow onto the shareholder's K-1 means the shareholder could pay taxes as high as 20% ($200,000). He also will owe state taxes on this money, and even at 5% that comes to him laying out another $50,000. Sneak in that Obama Care tax (up to 3.8%), and this knocks him down another $38,000.

The S corp. shareholder sees $712,000.00 after taxes on the million-dollar deal.

Which type of corporation you are and which you might like to become is up to you. I can only advise you that if you want to switch from a C to S, this will probably take the better part of two years. So get on this the minute you feel the inkling to sell your agency. There is plenty of good and bad to consider with both types of corporate structures, and I can't rightly tell you which is better for your specific purposes or if it is even smart for you to switch for your selling prospects. State taxation laws, the price of doing business, and the culture climate all differ from state to state. These factors, as many others, affect your taxation status.

Capital Gains

Here's where the government is going to be carefully looking into your affairs. Simply put, what you make from your sale—the capital gains—is taxable. This is why many a seller looks to keep that figure low and why a buyout, where a buyer pays a specific (smaller) amount over time, is so advantageous. Instead of getting your cool million in one big lump sum, you get smaller payments over time, and the IRS taxes you on this smaller amount. It has been my experience (and quite recently actually) where a seller has asked for an amendment to his contract, wherein I pay even less money each month, extending the payments over a longer period. The advantages for us both? The seller receives smaller payments (fewer capital gains) and has to pay the government less monthly, and RIGHTSURE gets to keep more money each month that we can invest back into our business. Of course changing horses midfield to a better tax advantage cannot work without that solid foundation of trust I mentioned, but should you be selling to someone you don't trust anyway?

What I outline above presents the lightest of toe touches into the deep waters of taxes. I don't propose to be an expert here, so hire those men and women who are, and they will help you swim deeper through what I have outlined here. But be sure you do your due diligence with taxes on both your buying and selling.

Chapter 8

The Good, the Bad, and the One That Got Away

"Three things man should not be content with:

With His opinions

With his character

With his spiritual condition

Three things with which a man should be content with:

With whatever happens

With friendships and possessions

With his pure thoughts"

James Allen, *Above Life's Turmoil*

Someone infinitely more interesting (love him or hate him) than me titled his book *The Art of the Deal*, which put me in mind of adding this section to this book and titling it "The Art of the Insurance Deal." In what I have presented so far, I have trickled in anecdotes of deals—some good, some bad—which I thought applicable to a point I was making. Here I'd like to take you through a few specific deals I have been involved in, some at the beginning of RIGHTSURE, some smack dab in the middle of our existence, and some not all that long ago to illustrate some of the concepts I mention in the above chapters.

I think what I learned in the art of each of these deals is pertinent both for buyer and seller.

It's Good to Be the Motorcycle & Scooter King

The first deal that comes to mind is one that defined RIGHTSURE in a specific way. It speaks to the concepts of consolidation, what it means to have a niche agency (and what you might expect from trying to sell one), how being the head of your agency might bode well for you when selling, the real power of a little human interaction, as well as never thinking a deal dead until papers are signed.

Back into owning my agency for the second time, I grew to want to become the specialists of specialists. RIGHTSURE was a personal liability broker, a niche shop already, but I wanted to get even more niche-y. In this pursuit and mindset, I began considering, researching, and in fact coming to acquire motorcycle insurance agencies. And in doing so I'd come to not only add greatly to our cache and cash flow but would come to be the "leader of the pack" (sorry, I couldn't help myself) writing policies on motorcycles, scooters, and Vespa scooters, specifically.

The big brokers were steering clear of insuring monoline motorcy-cles. They wanted the bigger premiums they'd get with car insurance policies; typically liability-only scooter and motorcycle policies ran between $75 to $140 tops, quite a low commission for those of us writing car insurance policies. But I did not have the checkbook at the time to chase car policies as the big boys did. And I didn't think this chase would be interesting in any way, shape, or form. Remember, for me, selling insurance is a highly creative act, and I err on the side of keeping what I do creative and challenging, best I can. I knew a little about motorcycles; my older brother rode them, did the Sturgis thing annually, etc. I even had had one at one time. I started gathering data about how to insure bikes, and made myself familiar with the language as well as everything else there was to know about them. But what drove me mostly was that I could approach this niche in a wholly different way and become the specialist of specialists.

The largest writer of California motorcycle insurance was a guy by the name of Mr. Mike Felder. Mike was referred to me, as he was looking to retire and, though he had four other buyers interested, I contacted him and put my hat (helmet in this case) into the ring. At the time Mike had over four thousand policies, a lucrative book for any potential buyer, and though I put a good offer on the table, in the end, it simply was not enough to buy his book. The deal "went dark," as we say, and that was the end of the story.

Well, not quite.

I am nothing if not tenacious. One of the most important lessons to learn in the art of the insurance deal, be you seller or buyer, is to never think a deal is done until papers have been signed. So a few months went by, and I figured, why not hit up Mike? I hadn't heard a thing about his deal going down—not that I'd be somebody he'd check in with—and I wanted that agency of his! Wouldn't you know it, none of those other four buyers could come to an agreement with Mike. My checking-in put me back in the running.

I told Mike I could be in San Francisco rather quickly and didn't want much more than an hour of his time, and he told me to come on up. Here was another valuable lesson learned—again as important to buyer and seller—"face time," meeting someone for even a quick cup of coffee, can make a real difference in negotiations . . . or at the very least, have the person pursuing the in-person meeting (me in this case) appear as a serious player in the deal.

I liked Mike even more in person than I had when talking to him over the phone. He had the most impressive shop. You know by now I am a "bells and whistles" kind of a guy; Mr. Technology, right? Well, when I walked into Mike's office, to see this successful man who is the king of motorcycle insurance, whose book is worth millions, and it's only Mike, a small desk, a laptop, his phone, and about fifteen file cabinets in his office, this is a guy that was hands-on in every aspect. He lived motorcycles, knew all there was to know about them, and subsequently how to write policies for them. He single-handedly changed the landscape of motorcycle insurance in California. He treated each of his many clients with a personal touch second to none and was on top of his game in a way few people I have ever met in this business are. Ah, the sole guy running things, as I said before, how great is that? Here I had only one super smart person to deal with, one man speaking for his agency. Because of the way Mike ran things, the deal would have few complications, if indeed I could get him to go for my deal.

I instantly got what Mike was after, understood fully where he was coming from, and he seemed to like me (our lunch took an hour and a half). He wanted to slip out of his work but have his clients retain the good service they were used to, basically keep everything the same without him having to be on the other end of the phone any longer. I told him I'd put together a Mike Felder tribute video for the net, assured him I wouldn't change a thing of what he was doing (why would I, he was so successful), and gave him a revised price. I shook Mike's hand at the end of our time together, told him I hoped we could do the deal, and wished him much luck in his retirement even if we couldn't.

I was about to board my plane a couple of hours later when Mike called and told me to resend the specifics of my offer before he had time to change his mind.

I bought his agency.

I won't kid you, Mike's deal saw me pay some of the highest multiples I ever paid for an agency—then as well as now—but his book and the way he did business was worth every dime I spent.

The second agency I bought in my rise to motorcycle insurance policy writing domination was from a supermodel in Arizona who was the biggest writer of bike policies in the area . . . and just too drop-dead beautiful for my own good. This was an instance where face time probably didn't serve me so well, as I was a bumbling, stumbling idiot in this stunning woman's presence. Dropping my coffee, thrusting my fingernail into the palm of her hand when I shook it, I was as uncool as you can get. But Jennifer Cartwright Peris couldn't have been nicer. She was smart as a whip and drove a solid bargain. I had to be on my toes about all her details, but in no time, as I had with

Mike, I came to an agreement with Jennifer despite how awestruck
I was at her physical presence.

Buying these two agencies put RIGHTSURE on the map. Consolidating into the motorcycle niche (remember me expounding on the
advantages to the seller about consolidating?), Mike and Jennifer's
lucrative books, the fact that not so many agencies were writing
motorcycle policies, and my desire to do so catapulted RIGHTSURE's
presence in the field. Yes, we took on considerable debt, but we
gained a much higher profile with funding institutions and banks as
I shouldered this new deal (I told you Mike's book required a large
investment) and we saw an uptick in policy volumes like never before.

Within twelve months we exceeded five thousand motorcycle
policies in force. A startlingly high amount when you consider an
average agency may insure 100 to 150 bikes at best. We were close
to rivaling those high-profile motorcycle dealerships who work their
insurance operations in-house.

Then Insure My Vespa was born.

After the motorcycle agency acquisitions, I realized nobody
was laser focused on writing policies for scooters, those Vespas I
mentioned earlier. I created insuremyvespa.com and quickly became
the undisputed insurance-writing king for scooters, a niche within a
niche within a niche.

How is that for specializing?

On top of all this, I became friends with Mike. I got to share in
his retirement adventures, relishing in his Facebook posts riding his

bike across the country, his wild few days spent in a Cuban hospital. We remain good friends to this day.

Playing with the Big Boys

As much as deals come my way these days from simply being in the game this long and having built a good reputation, I am still actively pursuing agencies. When I first bought my agency back, I was out there turning over a lot more rocks, but I will never stop in my pursuit of acquiring and getting into a good acquisition.

In what follows here, though, I was courted.

A large, publicly traded nationwide insurance conglomerate called in 2009 asking if I had an interest in purchasing their Personal Lines Division. They were looking to divest of this vertical in our regional area and wanted to focus on large commercial insurance offerings. They knew we had the financial capability to take the deal, and quite frankly I think they equated RIGHTSURE still with our prior bank relationship. This was in the early years of me getting the brokerage back, so maybe I still had the "stank of the bank" on me.

Somewhere along the line, I knew bank speak, understanding that culture would serve me.

This was perhaps the easiest deal I ever managed. The seller was so anxious to get out that they took what I had cash-in-hand and let me pay off the rest over thirty-six months, no questions asked, just happy to get the deal done.

What did I learn from this deal? First, here was a real example of the merits of having a good team in place to help with your selling.

This conglomerate had lawyers at the ready who had their papers drawn. With my team equal to the task, we made the deal happen even faster than I imagined. Second, this company knew exactly what they wanted, so there wasn't any real back and forth, maybe once or twice as I tweaked my terms, but not much more.

Surely, not everything a big corporation does applies to how we might conduct our business, but sometimes we can learn a lot from their efficiencies.

I learned even more in . . .

The $100 Million Deal

By now I know you are sick of reading the phrase "deep dive," but in this next deal—one that died halfway through happening—I learned so much that RIGHTSURE learned its best strokes for the deep dive we manage to this day. I also came to truly consider my company's culture, how important it is to me, and what I did and did not want for our future.

This deal played out between 2013 and 2014. RIGHTSURE was on a solid base by then, acquiring agencies, writing policies, being romanced by quite a few firms to consult. On a personal level, I was building myself back up to being a player in the field. Not a "player" in the sense of how I had acted all "Joe Cool"—like when I worked for the bank, but in the sense that my confidence was rising every day for what I could deliver. It had taken awhile to get back to how I felt before I sold my agency back in 1999, but five years in on my second time around, I was riding high back in the saddle.

And though I'm not an egotist, it did feel good to feel the full brush of my power returning.

I was engaged in a joint venture with a multibillion-dollar, multistate car seller with over one hundred dealerships across the United States. We had the technology in place and a solid reputation to become the sole car insurance brokerage for this company, and eventually we created a web platform with them to write what would come to be anywhere from one to three thousand policies a month. In fact, we created a separate LLC with this dealership to handle this specific business, an offshoot of RIGHTSURE. As I have mentioned in both the selling and buying chapters, there are plenty of ways to do a deal, and this joint venture proved quite lucrative.

Through this LLC, our reputation grew in this particular area, and with the car dealership specifically. In fact, we did so well with them, quite a few times they made offers to buy RIGHTSURE outright. I must say the offer on the table each time was quite healthy and the dealership was chomping at the bit to write me a check, but I wasn't up for selling to them . . . or anyone. Another lesson we can all learn: just because the money is on the table (and a lot of money at that) it doesn't mean the buyer/deal in question is the right one for you.

I was enjoying being the niche player I was, growing RIGHTSURE, being at the forefront of technology that was working around me daily. And as happens when you are good at what you do, when you start making money for not just yourself but someone else, RIGHTSURE became so well-known that soon we found ourselves in the mix of a deal with other big car dealerships and a multibillion-dollar communication company. This big brand, as well as those other dealerships, were in no way connected to the insurance business, but we all started on our way to acquiring funding to create an "insurance shell" that would allow us to write policies and eventually slip in other insurance brokers.

Big-time money was being considered here; the deal required us to raise $100 million. This was an amount that I had never been close to raising in any acquisition, let alone an amount I even would have considered going after. Frankly, I was far out of my comfort zone, above my pay grade, in up over the tips of my skis. It wasn't that I couldn't "speak the speak" and didn't enjoy flying around the country taking meetings, but a deal of this size didn't fit with my view of things. I had always been the one who made the ultimate decision to buy or not, for good or bad. Trying to gather up that much money, you invite lots of different people into the process, pretty much all alpha personalities trying to get their point across.

It was the cliché of too many queen bees and not enough worker bees made real.

This was a way of doing business, a culture if you will that didn't fit so well at RIGHTSURE. The sacrifices I saw coming down the pike for the greater good of simply adding more commas and zeros to our financials (sacrifices like having to let people go to make room for others, shifting divisions around) wasn't for me. What I had in RIGHTSURE then was malleable. I liked being able to provide my people with a secure living. We all liked each other, and my staff participated in our charity events and away-from-the-office outings with big smiles and a real desire to be together. I didn't want to mess with this.

In the end, we managed to raise half of the money needed, and then things started to gray around the edges. Although the projections for potential business were through the roof and became gospel pretty quickly, it was all just smoke and mirrors I soon saw (and in my background there is only one gospel). We all stood to make lots of money, but at any given time that projected amount fluctuated by who was projecting. When it comes to car dealerships specifically, there is a wide chasm between how much money they see in a single car sale and how much we make writing a policy. Selling a midlevel-priced car, almost immediately a car dealership sees a gross profit of many thousands per car; the first time we write the policy for that car, we see a commission from $60–$90. Yes, down the line things could get quite juicy for RIGHTSURE as future policies renewed, but this is just one small example of how projected earnings differ between parties, even if those parties happen to be in the same business.

The end of the deal came apart mostly because the players involved realized this was not turning out to be the proverbial match made in heaven. Queens not workers; more people—and money—involved, the more opinions we had on how things should be done. After $52 million was raised, all parties mutually agreed to stop additional capital raising and refocus on other core strategies, not involving insurance. We parted cordially (at least I did), and RIGHTSURE kept in business with that initial car dealership.

But as I said at the beginning of this story, I did learn a lot, even though the deal did not materialize. The deep dive (yes there is it again, sorry) that some of those other investors applied to their daily business was staggering to me. I thought RIGHTSURE applied technology intensely. I thought we picked through metrics, but these guys and girls, man, they raked through their sandboxes with fine-toothed combs! The way they looked at things made me stretch my approach in such a way that I knew I could never snap back to how I had been doing things. There is a great quote from Wayne Dyer that I will paraphrase here. He warns that when we stretch out that old pair of sweatpants so the elastic waistband no longer secures around our stomachs, those pants won't ever fit right again.

Once I stretched my mind to the possibilities of even more involved metrics and bigger and better technologies, I could never go back. Before this deal, I was comfortable looking at our sales, the specifics of deals, and the performance of my staff in what I felt was a meticulous way. After that big deal broke apart, I began applying the metrics I had seen used by those investors, never knowing I could go so deep. Not having been around those big players I would not have known these approaches even existed. Presently I employ ninety-two different metrics that are measured each night at midnight and, while enjoying my morning breakfast, those reports reveal every minute aspect of RIGHTSURE business. Being a junkie for this kind of stuff, you can imagine how much I love swimming in all those numbers and computer-generated reports.

The above deal took nearly a year of my life and was the biggest I had ever been involved in. It bolstered my confidence, brought the RIGHTSURE brand in front of lots of people who would never have known us, and had me sit in on meetings where I was once again acting like a sponge slurping up the good and the bad of investing and business on a level I had never known.

The One That Got Away

I think there's lots to be learned from the story of the best agency I NEVER bought.

When this lucrative shop came to sell, they had everything a buyer could ever want: loss reports from every one of their carriers; prior year ending carrier statements; prior month ending carrier statements; year to date and two prior years balance sheets and income statements. Their reporting went back from their inception and was so extensive and well documented that I couldn't ask of a single thing I needed to take my deep dive. They were asking for 2x revenue with a carve-out of their five largest commercial accounts to be paid at 75% of renewals for three years. It was the obligatory deal sent from heaven. The owner knew his value, knew the terms he wanted, and had all the information at the ready . . . lucky for the owner but unlucky for us. Buyers were lined up at his door to one-up each other's multiples. It was a veritable feeding frenzy.

RIGHTSURE stepped up to the plate on this one, but our offer was just shy of that full amount the seller was asking. And this seller wasn't going to consider even a penny less than he was asking; why should he? I have it on pretty accurate authority, though, that he received 2.25 times his prior year's revenue in ALL CASH up front and a renewal carve-out for his top five largest clients, precisely what he was asking for. Few sellers receive all cash up front these days, as most equity firms, banks, factoring firms, etc. prefer an owner carry up to as much as 30% and the buyer to have a minimum of 10 to 15% cash on hand. This seller got his full asking price and got out holding nothing. He simply presented a highly preferred agency with brand name preferred contracts, showing excellent loss ratios and more data than I have encountered from any other seller.

Yes, I would have loved to have bought him, and to this day I hate the fact that he got away. But this example as much illustrates that there are indeed good ones that even I can't catch as that you, as a seller, can get lots of what you want if you manage your own due diligence and present such an attractive commodity to the buyer that they simple can't refuse you in a bidding war you come to engineer.

Chapter 9

RIGHTSURE Consulting: For Buyer or Seller

"When you change the way you look at things, the things you look at change."

Wayne Dyer

Increasingly over the last year, I have been approached by both buyers and sellers for counsel\feedback\advice. With so many acquisitions under my belt, buying agencies is something I not only feel I can do but also something I can certainly give good counsel about. It's been my experience that when hiring someone from outside your team—be that the seller or buyer's team—the consultant can bring a new perspective to documents that need to be written and signed, as much as fresh ideas on how to conduct some due diligence that maybe nobody has yet to consider.

The general inquiry I get most from folks looking to sell or buy, or coming to consider either one, is one of general direction and guidance surrounding the process. I have even developed an abbreviated fee schedule based upon my love for our industry and consulting. My fees are inexpensive, and I consult for both buy and sell side transactions, with the fee based upon the premium volume of the agency.

The consulting process involves a series of standards and benchmarks about sale and purchase process. With few exceptions—so few I can't think of any as I come to write this—the points below are what both seller and buyer must mostly concern themselves with (for different reasons, of course) when it comes to agency acquisition.

Here are the points I touch upon in my consulting.

First, the participants must make an independent review of the sales price based on a multiple of revenue or EBITDA valuation. From both the seller's point of view and the buyers' (granted two opposite ends of the coin), this valuation is most important. I won't kid you that both parties will present the same number the first time they sit down at the table, but eventually they must settle on a valuation from their specific deep dives. In my consulting, I show **how to conduct a deep dive into valuation**, be you a seller or buyer.

Many documents will come from the process of buying and selling, born as much from each side's research and experts and created during negotiations as birthed whole cloth in the contract created. I provide insight into each piece of paper, whether you presently have it front of you or not, advise you on what to expect and also what documents are absolutely needed at the seller, buyer, and carrier level. Yes, it's a lot of details, but I can steer you through it all . . . because I have been through it all.

First, I will help you create, decipher, and all-around assist you with a: **Detailed Letter Of Intent**.

In the RIGHTSURE world, we often get out a letter of intent within a day from vetting a buyer's proposal. This happens as quick as it does because when we come to buy, we pretty much have looked across the seller's website, taken a peek at the revenue breakdown they have sent us, and have taken a gander at who the agency's carriers are. We know fully well how lucrative this potential acquisition could be for us. It behooves RIGHTSURE to get things going quickly if we indeed want the agency and are looking to freeze the deal (not that a seller can't take our letter of intent and shop other deals . . . which I told you happens quite a bit with RIGHTSURE acquisitions). It's simply good business, I believe, to present that letter of intent ASAP, as it solidifies a buyer's intention to the seller.

Now, as much as I can help the seller draft this letter, I can also help the buyer in how to best read this letter and come to a clear realization of their value assessment. When a buyer comes back to the seller with their letter of intent, the buyer needs to know what they are reading and why the numbers fall out the way they do. As I have mentioned, often our deep dive brings us to a number higher than the seller even considered, and if this is true, though thrilled, the buyer will want to know how we came to the number we did.

Carriers and vendors will see other breakdowns specific to them as the deal progresses, but that's for later. The letter of intent is intended for the eyes of the seller and buyer and their team only; it's not to be shared with anyone else.

Another part and parcel of what I consult on is the **Offer** and the **Acceptance Agreements**. Drawing up these papers, which are akin to the Bill of Sale when buying a car, can take some time and consideration. The specifics of the impending deal will be outlined here, the nuts and bolts beyond the broad strokes sketched out in the letter of intent, and these are the papers that will be shared and submitted to the carriers involved. There is bound to be some back and forth at this stage—from seller or buyer or both. But I assure you, the advice I give here, even combing through the various facts and figures that might be presented, chugs along a lot quicker than when the lawyers get their hands on all these pages. Those legal expert men and women have to earn their commissions, after all, as they typically take a couple of weeks to go through this stuff. I will at least have you understanding fully what you are giving and getting.

With the sale imminent, vendors—phone and Internet suppliers, the alarm company, etc.—will need to be notified. We can help draft and consider the **Assignment** and **Assumptions Agreements**, notifying these third parties pretty much at the same time buyer and seller sign off on the sale. It's not just the carriers and clients who need to learn about the sale and who might get paid in the future if the vendors are kept on after the acquisition.

As you read, I had an all-too-painful learning experience in failing to execute a simple UCC filing on one of my sellers. Managing this all-important Uniform Commercial Code examination is mandatory, I feel, and as part of my consulting, I give **UCC Filing Guidance.** Learn sooner rather than later if your seller is beholden to anyone else with bank levies or other significant debts. And buyers, find out if a partner has committed your assets someplace else. This actually happened in a deal I was into after I learned from a UCC filing that one partner had levied assets of the agency unbeknownst to the other partner.

At the end of the acquisition, as I indicated in my behind-the-scenes section, a lot needs to happen immediately following the sale . . . for seller and buyer both. In my consulting, I've come in to help handle **Post Transaction Compliance** and **Reconciliation** for both parties.

Certainly, many sellers simply want to walk away, throw their keys over their shoulder, and say bye-bye after the papers are signed. But I can assure you, the seller will be getting at least two to three calls a week for the next sixty to ninety days, depending on how much he or she cleans up before the sale. We consult on what to do to make the post transition for the seller as painless as it can be.

On the buyer's side of things, from my constant involvement in the post-game wrap-up, so to speak, I am certainly the person who can head things off at the pass, giving good counsel before the sign over of the agency. Simply put, the buyer needs to know how to follow his or her money from the agency they just bought, how to get a system in place for reconciliation and compliance, and how to right the flow of funds to where they should be going.

You might not even be ready to sell your agency or might be considering buying one. On the other hand, you might be in the middle of negotiations or setting up your team to start the process of jumping into the buying or selling of an agency. As much as I am always in the market for a new acquisition, I am also always ready to consult on one.

Conclusion

"To Sell or Not to Sell" and Who to Sell To

"A good character is the best tombstone. Those who loved you and were helped by you will remember you when forget-me-nots have withered. Carve your name on hearts, not on marble."
Charles Spurgeon

So, are you ready to sell? And what's more, ready to sell to me?

I won't kid you; I liked imparting the wisdom in this book (if you will see it as that and not just me bragging). I do indeed love talking about as much as working this business we are in. But at the end of the day, I want your sale and many others to cross my desk. They might not all be good for me and RIGHTSURE, or they may become something different after we come to structure the deal differently. But I at least want a crack at what you are selling. From all you have read, I doubt you'll be knocking at my door trying to sell me your health insurance agency; you know where my bread has been buttered now for the past twenty-seven years. But you also know that I am interested in my niche as it applies to so many aspects of insurance, and I am always considering how to invest some new technology into an aspect of insurance that I might not have thought of before.

Years of hard work have allowed me to come to this place and give you my story, maybe help you a bit with your considerations and possibly present myself as the buyer you will want to sell to. As you realize by now, I don't have the time, energy, and mostly I *do not* have the inclination to keep secrets to myself about selling and buying. It's always been my credo—and one you certainly realize loud and clear after reading this book—to wish for a seller to be well-versed, heavily armed with experts, and know his or her stuff when it comes time that they are sitting down across a negotiation from me. The process goes that much smoother when everybody is well-informed, and we can all get through negotiations quickly.

If you decide that I am not the buyer for you or I can't come to the deal you want or, after crunching my stats I realize your agency won't be right for me, no harm no foul, I say. As you have read, I have been in the midst of deals that took months and months to fit together, only to have them not come to fruition in the end. I don't consider these instances a waste of time, and I hope even if you get up to bat but don't connect a few times yourself that you won't think all those experiences a waste of your time either.

I realize, as the buyer, I have the advantage. I know many a seller is looking to get out as fast as they can by the time they put their agency up for sale, and other owners are simply burned out. You might fall in either category or in the middle someplace with how you are feeling presently looking to get your agency sold, or at least mulling over the idea to sell. A lot of pressures come to the seller, I know. But take my advice from the above, make sure the deal you come to is the right deal for you, try the best you can to submerge emotion in all this, let the numbers drive the deal, and don't be hasty.

Nothing makes me happier than to turn right around after doing our deep diving over facts and figures to find that an agency might be worth more than its owner, the seller, has priced it. This is a win-win for everybody; the seller can potentially make more money than he or she ever thought possible, and I have found an agency that I want for sure!

For those especially in the throes of selling or getting ready, you already know much of what you read here. I make no claims for guru-like insights or imparting heretofore unknown secrets of how to sell an agency. I am not reinventing the wheel here. Much of what I imparted, beyond the personal stuff, you can find in other sources. That old Internet is a wealth of information when selling and buying, and surely by now you have either hired your team or are about to go look for a good accountant and lawyer to see you through the process. I thought maybe if you heard some solid facts from a guy who is out there currently acquiring agencies, it might benefit you. I hope I have added to your knowledge here, if even a little bit.

Let's recap then what I have tried to retrofit into your worldview. I'll be brief, but I think these big bullet points bear repeating. I jump around a bit below, as much to keep me on my toes as to keep you interested as I more or less repeat myself.

- <u>No two deals are alike</u>. Yes, that agency you built is unique. It has the stamp of your particular personality and work ethic upon it. You nurtured the seed, cultivated the land, and worked hard to bring the crop to full bloom. Why then wouldn't the deal you come to present answer your needs and wishes? I respect the terms of any buyer, from what is set across a contract to what he or she wishes beyond what we sign off on. Rely on your team to help you see your wishes made into reality.

- <u>Speaking of that team, hire them . . . and fast.</u> You are going to need people around you that you can trust, who are experts and who will, at times, tell you the hard truths, even if it goes beyond your feelings.

- And about those feelings: it's good to have them; let your gut guide you, but at the end of the day remember, <u>the numbers are what drives the deal</u> . . . at least they are for me.

- <u>Time is of the essence, so start investing hours, and money if you have to, in making your agency ready to sell.</u> The earlier you realize you might be ready to retire or get the inkling that you might be in the market for selling, see to those things I mentioned way back when to make your agency more lucrative to a buyer. Certainly, all that I advise won't apply, and some won't be feasible for you to implement, but getting your ducks in a row will make your agency more attractive to potential buyers.

- Following from this, I do advise <u>letting technology in the door if you have yet to or updating stuff around the office best you can.</u> Yes, I know I am a nut for this stuff, but even dipping your toe in the water of updating via the digital space won't hurt you, and in many cases, could very well help. The more you know of the online world will help you come to <u>vet your potential buyers.</u>

- <u>A little study of insurance history (beyond my chapter 3) will benefit you.</u> Certainly, learning a bit about the old ways of selling opposed to the new will come in handy now. According to the great American writer James Baldwin: "If you know whence you came, there are absolutely no limitations to where you can go." To which I like to add British author and satirist Terry Pratchett's quip: "If you don't know where you come from, then you don't know where you are, and if you don't know where you are, then you don't know where you're going. And if you don't know where you're going, you're probably going wrong."

- <u>Find that "why" if you can.</u> It might no longer apply to your business, but now that you are getting out, might you consider the why of your worldview, or at least where you might be traveling next down the road of life. How does this help in your selling? I dare say, if you have a pretty good reason for why you are selling, you might be able to fashion a deal—staying in to still work your handful of clients while a new owner takes over the day-to-day operations and headaches, getting out entirely with a one lump sum—for exactly what serves your why best. But remember, although it is tempting to do this, keep those retirement plans as subtext in the deal. <u>You shouldn't determine your selling price solely on your perceived retirement needs.</u> The amount you think you need to jump on the Harley and speed off into the sunset is immaterial to the value of your agency. *

- I come from a generation taught not to discuss sex, religion, politics, or money in polite conversation. But right now I need to impress upon you to <u>get your financials in order</u>. Whether that means cleaning up some debt, downsizing the shop, consolidating, or going over your statements with a fine-tooth comb so you know exactly what you are bringing to the table, now is the time to make sure your money is in order.

- <u>Clean Up That Partnership.</u> For those of you in a partnership (or answerable to stockholders), make sure you have things well considered and completely figured where other owners and money people are concerned. I can't tell you the horror stories I have heard about deals being readied and about to be signed, only to be stopped because a contingent from the agency or a partner halts the proceedings.

- <u>Shhh!</u> Keep your intentions about selling and certainly the terms of the sale as quiet as you can, for as long as you can. Yes, it will come out after time that you are selling, especially among your employees and agencies in your niche, but try to play things as close to your chest as possible at all times. Nobody needs to know your business save for you and the buyer.

And last:

As good old Clint Eastwood warned us way back in one of the early *Dirty Harry* movies, "A man has got to know his limitations." Apply this caution to the selling of your agency. Consider the current marketplace when you are running your numbers. Look at your agency from as objective an angle as you can and consider your shop honestly: do you insure low or high-risk clients; is your niche seemingly healthy;

are you an independent or captive agency; and who are your carriers? It behooves you to be as honest as you can, presenting the warts and all (at least in the mirror to yourself) so you know exactly what you are offering at the end of the day.

I want you to find the best fit for your agency, to get the right price for that which you spent so much time putting your heart, soul, and time into. It betters our industry if standards are maintained, if a seller feels confident in their buyer, if their trust is born from the deals we do, if we keep our industry healthy. I wholeheartedly believe insurance is the backbone of American business in many ways, and even if you are about to get out of our business, you did contribute to it at one time, bolstering our country's economy in some fashion. And I believe, truly, that there is value in that.

I hope you find what you are looking for out there, sellers and buyers both. Keep your possibilities open, listen to your experts (and consultants), and do indeed push for what you want. My job here has not been to convince you as much as it was to clarify. I hope that through what you see from us and what you read here that you come to recognize that RIGHTSURE is indeed doing things as positively as we can, with caring for people always at our core.

www.ingramcontent.com/pod-product-compliance
Lightning Source LLC
Chambersburg PA
CBHW071855200326
41519CB00016B/4393